YOU HAVEN'T READ AT ALL . . .

What's the best way to make a bull sweat?

Give him a tight jersey.

What's the difference between a vitamin and a hormone?

You can't hear a vitamin.

What's the cannibal's favorite religious text?

How to Serve Your Fellow Man.

UNTIL YOU READ GROSS JOKES!

BESTSELLERS FOR EVERYONE!

GROSS JOKES (1244, $2.50)
by Julius Alvin
You haven't read at all—until you read GROSS JOKES! This complete compilation is guaranteed to deliver the sickest, sassiest laughs!

TOTALLY GROSS JOKES (1333, $2.50)
by Alvin Julius
From the tasteless ridiculous to the taboo sublime, TOTALLY GROSS JOKES has enough laughs in store for even *the most* particular humor fanatics.

MUNICH 10 (1300, $3.95)
by Lewis Orde
They've killed her lover, and they've kidnapped her son. Now the world-famous actress is swept into a maelstrom of international intrigue and bone-chilling suspense—and the only man who can help her pursue her enemies is a complete stranger. . . .

PAY THE PRICE (1234, $3.95)
by Igor Cassini
Christina was every woman's envy and every man's dream. And she was compulsively driven to making it—to the top of the modeling world and to the most powerful peaks of success, where an empire was hers for the taking, if she was willing to PAY THE PRICE.

GROSS JOKES
By Julius Alvin

ZEBRA BOOKS
KENSINGTON PUBLISHING CORP.

ZEBRA BOOKS

are published by

KENSINGTON PUBLISHING CORP.
475 Park Avenue South
New York, N.Y. 10016

NINTH PRINTING

Printed in the United States of America

In fond memory of Helen Keller

CONTENTS

Chapter One:

REVOLTING RACIAL AND ETHNIC JOKES

A store in Harlem displayed a collection of toupees for Negro men. An elderly man wandered in and couldn't help asking, "What are those things made of?"

The salesman smiled. "They're woven from the real pussy hair of white women."

A gleam came in the old man's eye. "I'll take one," he said.

"Shall I wrap it for you?" the clerk asked.

"No, I'll eat it here."

———————

Why do Negroes have sex on the brain all the time?

Because their heads are covered with pubic hair.

Saint Peter was logging in new arrivals at the gates of heaven when he saw a black guy from a small town in Mississippi standing in front of him.

"What do you think you're doing here?" Saint Peter demanded.

"You mean black folk aren't allowed in?" the man asked.

"Only very special blacks. What makes you think you qualify?"

The man pulled himself up. "I'm the very first black man from my town to marry a white woman."

"When did you do that?" Saint Peter asked.

The black guy looked down at his watch. "About five minutes ago."

———————

The black man had been shot in the lower leg in a barroom fight. The ambulance took him to the hospital emergency room, where the doctor cut off his pants at the knee. To his amazement, the head of his cock stuck out one of the slits, and the doctor and the ambulance attendant began laughing.

The black man looked up angrily and said, "You can laugh, motherfuckers, but if you'd been shot, your prick would shrink, too."

———————

Why did the black Muslim stop eating his wife?

He heard some dude call her a pig.

One engine of an airplane went out over the Rockies, and the pilot found himself unable to maintain altitude. He turned to the three passengers on board and said, "Sorry. One of you is going to have to jump out to save the rest of us. I can't go because I have to fly the plane. So I'll ask each of you a question and the first one to give a wrong answer has to jump. Okay?"

The men reluctantly agreed.

The pilot asked the first man, a professor, "What was the greatest maritime disaster in history?"

"The sinking of the Titanic."

"Right," the pilot said. Then he asked the second man, a congressman, "How many people from the Titanic died?"

The congressman guessed, "About 1500."

"Very good," the pilot said. Then he turned to the third passenger, a Negro. "Okay, boy. Name them."

———————————

The telephone rang at the Mississippi office of the NAACP. The secretary was out to lunch, so the treasurer answered.

"Hello there, boy," a voice drawled. "Put me through to the head nigger."

Enraged, the treasurer snapped, "What makes you think you can talk to me like that?"

"Listen, boy," the caller said. "I wanna contribute $100,000 to yer cause, so y'all kin just put me through to your head nigger."

"Hold de line, boss," the treasurer replied. "I thinks I see dat jigaboo comin' in de door right now."

A Puerto Rican and a white guy were standing on a tenement roof. The white turned to the Puerto Rican and said, "The updrafts on the side of this building are terrific. Watch." The white guy jumped off the side of the building, fell to within three feet of the sidewalk and floated back up, landing on his feet on top of the building.

The Puerto Rican was so impressed he decided to try it. He took a flying leap off the side and a few seconds later splattered all over the sidewalk below.

Two cops were watching from across the street. One shook his head and said to the other, "Boy, that Clark Kent sure hates Puerto Ricans."

Why did God make Adam white?

Did you ever try to take a rib from a black dude?

The black dude heard about the contest to judge the biggest penis, with a 25 pound turkey as a prize. His wife didn't want him to enter, but he went anyway. A little later, he came home with the turkey. His wife, still embarrassed, asked, "You didn't take that big black thing out in public, did you?"

He answered, "Only enough to win."

Three women died and went to heaven. At the Pearly Gates, Saint Peter asked each what she had died from.

"Cancer," said the first woman.

"Diabetes," said the second.

"Gonorrhea," said the third, a foxy black chick.

"Gonorrhea?" said Saint Peter. "Young people like you don't die from gonorrhea."

"When you gives it to a man like Leroy, you does!"

———————

A Japanese diplomat was called back to Tokyo for a lengthy consultation. When he returned to New York, he heard rumors that his attractive young wife had been frequenting the jazz scene and getting friendly with the musicians.

"Yoshiko," the proper diplomat admonished, "have you been diluting your cultural heritage by consorting with black musicians?"

"Akio," answered his wife, "why you laying such a motherfucking, jive ass trip on me?"

———————

What's Scotland?

A place where men are men and sheep are nervous.

———————

What's the difference between a JAP and a job?

Most jobs suck after 20 years.

What's the difference between a JAP and a killer whale?

Killer whales eat seamen.

———————————

What's the difference between a JAP and jello?

Jello moves when you eat it.

———————————

What's a Greek gentleman?

A man who takes a girl out three times before he propositions her brother.

———————————

The Polack was put to work on the chain saw on his first day at the lumber yard. He'd been working about ten minutes when the foreman heard him shout, "Ouch!"

The foreman came running over and asked, "What happened?"

"I don't know," the Polack said, "I just stuck my hand out like this and . . . oops, there goes the other one."

A Jewish boy came home from college and sat down to have a heart-to-heart talk with his doting mother. "I've got some good news and some bad news," he said. "The bad news is that I'm a homosexual."

"Oh, no!" his mother exclaimed.

"Before you faint," the son continued, "the good news is I'm in love with a doctor."

———————

The Italian immigrant went to the doctor to complain that he wasn't sure how to make his new wife pregnant. After struggling with language problems, the doctor simplified his advice—just stick your longest thing where your wife is hairiest.

Two months later, the Italian came back to complain that it didn't work. "I've been sticking my nose in her armpit every night," he said, "and nothing's happened."

———————

What's the difference between a Polish woman and a hockey goalie?

A hockey goalie changes his pads every three periods.

———————

What do they call an abortion in Prague?

A cancelled Czech.

What do you call an uncircumcised Jewish baby?

A girl.

The nurse walked into the emergency room, where the Polack was stretched out. She saw his horribly swollen, bright red genitals and asked, "What in the hell happened to him?"

Another nurse explained, "He got the directions of his doctor all wrong. The doctor told him to *prick* his *boil*."

Where can you buy panties made out of fertilizer bags and bras made out of beer cans?

Fredericks of Poland.

Two Norwegians were sitting at a bar for nearly an hour. Finally, one turned to the other and said, "You know, Arnie, I've been thinking. It's a dog-eat-dog world."

Arnie turned away and contemplated for another hour. Then he turned back to his friend and said, "Maybe it is. Or it could be the other way around."

An American woman, a French woman, and a Russian woman were in the lingerie department buying panties for a trip. The sales clerk turned to the American woman and asked how many pairs she'd need.

"Seven," she replied. "One pair for each day of the week."

Next came the French woman, who said she'd need five pair. "One for each day Monday through Friday. I am with my lover on the weekend and I don't wear panties."

The saleswoman wrote the order down, then turned to the Russian woman to ask how many pairs she'd need.

"Twelve," she answered. "January, February, March . . ."

————————

What does the sign above the urinal in a Polish men's room say?

Please don't eat the big white mints.

————————

What happened to the Polish terrorist who tried to blow up a bus?

He burnt his lips on the exhaust pipe.

A brick fell on the Polack's head at a construction site, and when he came to, the doctor gave him an association test.

"Wife," the doctor said.

"Natalie," the man replied.

"Mother," the doctor said.

"Sophie."

"Brother."

"Stash."

"Good," the doctor said. "Now, daughter."

"Coathanger," the Polack replied.

What's the difference between a rich Polack and a poor Polack?

Whitewalls on their wheelbarrows.

The Polack was out driving with his new girlfriend. Every time they came to a light, he put his hand on her thigh, and she slapped it away. Finally, determined to get somewhere, he jammed his hand under her skirt and all the way into her cunt. She screamed so loudly that he inadvertently stomped on the accelerator. The car shot forward and slammed into a tree.

When the Polack regained consciousness, he turned to his moaning girlfriend and asked, "Are you hurt?"

"Yes," she groaned. "I'm slit from asshole to belly button."

"I know," he said, "I got my whole hand inside. But are you hurt?"

How many canaries can you get under a Scotsman's kilt?

It depends how long the perch is.

A Polack who'd recently come to the United States walked into a bar one day carrying a pistol, a bag of shit, and a dead cat. He asked the bartender for a shot of rye. He downed the whiskey, picked up the pistol, and fired three shots into the bag of shit. Then he picked up the dead cat and started gnawing.

The bartender asked the Polack what in the hell he thought he was doing.

"I want to be like American man," the Polack said. "Drink whiskey, shoot the shit, and eat pussy."

Why don't Polish women breast-feed their children?

It hurts too much to boil their nipples.

Why did the Polish woman with the huge cunt douche with Crest?

She heard it reduced cavities.

How can you recognize an Italian airline?

The planes have hair under the wings.

_____

What happened to the Polish guy who didn't pay his garbage bill?

They stopped delivering.

_____

Why don't Polish workers get lunch breaks?

Because they'd have to retrain afterwards.

_____

How can you tell an Italian cesspool?

It's the one with the diving board.

_____

What equipment do they issue to Polish sewer workers?

Straws.

Why did the Polish guy wrap his hamster in electrical tape?

So it wouldn't explode when he fucked it.

One day while relieving himself in a public restroom, Bill noticed the unusually long penis on the black guy next to him. "How do you guys get such long dicks?" he asked.

"Exercise," the black guy said. "When we have sex, we push it in slow, and pull it out quick. That stretches it."

Bill promised himself he'd try the method that night. Shortly after he and his wife made love, Bill asked, "Did you notice anything different?"

"Yeah," his wife said. "You fuck like a nigger."

Why was the black man acquitted of rape on the grounds of temporary insanity?

Because his cock was so big that when he got an erection, it cut off the flow of blood to his brain.

A young Irishman went to a whorehouse for the first time. When he told the madam he was a virgin, she showed him how to put on a rubber, rolling it down on her thumb. The young man trotted upstairs. After he fucked the girl, she said, "That rubber must have broken. I feel all wet inside." The Irishman held up his thumb and said, "No, it didn't. It's just as good as new."

Chapter Two:

APPALLING ANIMAL JOKES

Every day the man came into the grocery store at lunchtime, bought a big can of dog food, went across the street to a bench in the park, and ate the dog food with a spoon. His strange habit was noticed by a doctor who regularly walked through the park. One day the doctor came up to the man and said, "You know, that stuff isn't good for you. It can kill you."

The man shrugged. "I've been eating it every day for twenty years."

The doctor repeated the warning, but to no avail. A month or so later, he noticed the man wasn't on the bench for a couple of days in a row. Another park regular told him the man had died.

"I told him that dog food would kill him," the doctor said.

"It wasn't the dog food," the man said. "He was sitting on the curb licking his dick and a truck ran over him."

A rural farmer was a sex maniac, but he was so ugly that no woman would come near him. So he went around the countryside fucking every animal he saw. One day another farmer saw him fucking one of his cows. He came over to the field and called out, "You crazy bastard! One of these days you're going to end up fucking yourself to death."

About a month and a half later, the same farmer was walking down the road when he saw the sex maniac lying in the bushes. It seemed that the man was dead. The farmer walked over and laughed, saying aloud, "I told him he'd fuck himself to death."

All of a sudden the sex maniac's eyes opened. "Quiet!" he hissed. He pointed upward, a look of lust in his eyes as he added, "There's a gorgeous buzzard circling up there."

———————————

What's the shepherd's favorite song?

"I'm in love with ewe . . . ewe . . . ewe."

The herder came into town after six months with his flock. He headed straight for the local whorehouse. When he got up to a room, the whore asked him what scent he wanted her to use.

He handed her a paper bag. "I brought my favorite," he said.

She opened the bag and recoiled at the odor. "What is this?"

"Sheep shit."

What did the rich wool merchant do with the expensive fur coat?

He gave it to his favorite little lamb.

Spring had almost arrived, and one herder turned to the other and said, "Boy, I can't wait until shearing time is here."

"Why, so you can get a chance to get back into town and have some fun?"

"No. So I can finally see them naked."

Two guys were walking down the street when they saw a dog licking his dick. "Boy," one guy said. "I wish I could do that."

"You probably could," the other guy replied. "But you'd probably have to pet him a little first."

The keeper was walking through the zoo one night when he saw one of his chimpanzees screwing the daylights out of a giraffe. He was so amazed that the next night he watched until the monkey made his way to the hippo's cage and mounted that huge beast. On the third night, after the chimp fucked a lioness, he captured the animal and brought it home to tell the amazing tale to his wife. But when he walked into the bedroom with the chimp in hand, his wife sat up in bed and shrieked, "No, George. Get that fucking sex maniac out of here!"

———————

What's Spanish Human?

A new insecticide that makes flies so horny they screw themselves to death.

———————

Why do dogs lick their genitals?

Because they can.

———————

What's the best way to make a bull sweat?

Give him a tight jersey.

There wasn't much social life in the small Southern town, so when the new schoolteacher was invited for dinner at the apartment of another female teacher, she finally got up the courage to ask, "What do you do for sex around here?"

"I'll show you," the older teacher replied. She whistled and a Great Dane bounded into the room. She lifted her skirt and the Dane began lapping furiously at her cunt. After a while, however, the dog began to get an erection and tried to mount. The teacher slapped him hard across the face and ordered him out of the room.

"I don't understand," the younger woman said. "That prick of his looked so inviting. Why don't you let him fuck you?"

"Are you kidding? With all those kids to deal with every day, the last thing I want to do when I come home is deal with puppies!"

Two herders found themselves a particularly attractive ewe one afternoon. One of them had just climbed on and started humping when the sheep stuck its tongue out.

"Damn," the other herder exclaimed. "Your prick is coming out the other end."

"Then stick another sheep on!"

Where does virgin wool come from?

From sheep the herder couldn't catch.

An Australian missionary was dragged out of bed by some very angry aborigines one night. Before he knew what was happening, he was tied to a post. "What's going on?" he asked.

The aborigine chief said, "One of our women just gave birth to a white baby. Since you're the only white man in many days' walk, you have to die."

The missionary called the chief close and said, "I want to remind you of one thing, Chief. You know that flock of pure white sheep I keep? Well, one of them gave birth to a black lamb, and there aren't any other black sheep around."

The aborigine looked thoughtful for a moment, then barked a command to have the missionary cut free. As the cleric was rubbing his wrists, the chief whispered, "I keep your secret, you keep mine."

What did the girl say to the centipede crawling across her cunt?

No, no, a thousand times no.

An American, an Irishman, and a Scotsman were confined to a rural hospital after an automobile crash. They'd been laid up for over two weeks when they saw a flock of sheep being driven by.

"God," the American said, "I wish one of those ewes was Bo Derek."

"I wish one was my lovely wife Colleen," the Irishman said.

"I wish it was dark!" the Scotsman exclaimed.

An Australian down on his luck was forced to sign up for a year's stint working on a giant sheep ranch in the outback. There must have been fifty men working on the ranch, but not a single woman. "What do you do for sex?" he asked the ranch boss.

The man smiled. "Wait until five o'clock. You'll see."

Finally, five o'clock came and the men suddenly began racing toward the sheep corral. The new hand stopped the foreman and said, "Now I understand what you do for sex. But why are they in a hurry? There's over a hundred sheep in that one corral."

"They don't want to get an ugly one."

A man was in a bar complaining that his wife paid five times as much attention to their German shepherd as she did to him.

"Well, that's not unusual," the bartender said reassuringly. "You're at work all day, and pets are good company."

"Good company, hell," the man said. "I came home early the other night and found her douching with Gravy Train."

———————————

A woman came to a podiatrist with a complaint that her feet always hurt. He immediately noticed that she was extremely bowlegged. He asked if she'd always been that way.

"No," she said. "Not until recently. I've been fucking a lot doggie fashion."

"Well, I think you're going to have to stop."

"I can't," she replied. "That's the only way my German shepherd fucks."

On a trip to Australia, a woman fell madly in love with a kangaroo. Disregarding the warnings of her tour guide, she had an aborigine witch doctor perform a wedding ceremony, then returned to the states with her husband.

Sure enough, three months later she and the kangaroo were in the office of a marriage counselor. "I think I can diagnose the problem right away," the counselor said. "You obviously can't establish any kind of communication with a kangaroo."

"That isn't the problem," the woman said. "We get along fine except in bed. There it's nothing but hop on, hop off, hop on, hop off."

Chapter Three:

OFFENSIVE JUVENILE JOKES

A five-year-old boy was accused of making a teenage girl pregnant. In court, the mother pleaded with the judge that her son couldn't possibly have done it. She unzipped the boy's fly, exposing his penis. "Look, your honor," she said. "See how tiny his organ is. He couldn't possibly have—"

"Mother, please," the boy whispered urgently, "if you don't stop stroking it, we're sure to lose this case."

Little Jimmy was hanging up his dad's coat when a package of condoms fell out. "What are these for?" he asked.

His father stammered, then said, "They're to keep my cigarettes dry."

The next day Jimmy walked into a drugstore and asked the clerk for a package of Trojans. "What size would you like?" the clerk asked with amusement.

"Oh, big enough to fit a Camel," the boy replied.

The twelve-year-old boy marched into the whorehouse and asked the madam, "Do any of your whores have V.D.?" The lady looked at him and said, "Get the hell out of here." So he acted as if he was leaving, but when her back was turned, he sneaked upstairs. He went around to all the whores asking if they had V.D., and they all said, "Get the hell out of here, little boy."

He was about to leave when he saw one last whore sitting in the corner, looking sad. So he went up to her and asked, "Do you have V.D.? I want to fuck you so I can get V.D."

"Get out of here," she said.

"Do you have V.D.?" he kept asking. Finally, she said yes. And eventually he persuaded her to go with him. Afterwards, she asked him why the hell he wanted to get V.D.

He replied, "So when I go home and fuck my babysitter, she'll get V.D. And when my father takes her home and fucks her, he'll get V.D. Then when he fucks my mother, she'll get V.D. And then, when my mother puts out for the mailman, he'll get V.D. And he's the son-of-a-bitch who stepped on my frog!"

———————————

A little girl watched her father take a shower. She asked him about his testicles. He told her, "Those are my apples."

Quickly the child scooted away and told her mother what Daddy said. The mother replied, "Did Daddy tell you about the dead limb they're hanging on to?"

An eight-year-old came into the house one day and announced, "Mommy, Janie and I want to get married."

Amused, his mother replied, "If you and Janie should get married, what will you do for money?"

"Oh, that's okay. You and Daddy give me money. Janie gets money from her mommy and daddy."

Still continuing the jest, the mother said, "When a boy and a girl get married, they have children. Then what will you do?"

The boy shrugged and said, "So far Janie and I have been lucky."

———————

The little girl asked her mother, "Mommy, how was Johnny across the street born?"

The mother said, "Well, the stork brought him."

"So how was Jenny next door born?"

"The stork brought her, too."

"Shit," the little girl said, "doesn't anybody fuck around this neighborhood?"

———————

What's the definition of a crummy bastard?

A little boy eating crackers in church while his mother and father are getting married.

Two young boys went into the drugstore and picked up two boxes of tampons. When they took them to the counter, the clerk asked, "Are these for your mother, boys?"

"Nope," one boy replied. "We just heard about how if you used this, you could ride horses and go swimming and do a lot of other neat things."

––––––––––––––––––

"Mommy, Mommy, what are vampires?"

"Don't ask questions. Just drink your blood."

––––––––––––––––––

"Mommy, Mommy, I'm not hungry."

"Shut up and eat your soup before it clots."

––––––––––––––––––

"Mommy, Mommy, why is Grandma so pale?"

"Shut up and keep digging."

––––––––––––––––––

"Mommy, Mommy, I'm running around in a circle."

"Quiet, or I'll nail your other foot to the floor."

"Mommy, Mommy, Daddy just drowned my puppy!"

"Don't cry, dear. Maybe he had to do it."

"No, he didn't. He promised me I could."

"Mommy, Mommy, what happened to your scabs?"

"Shut up and eat your corn flakes."

"Mommy, Mommy, are you sure this is the way to make pizza?"

"Shut up and get back into the oven."

"Mommy, Mommy, Daddy's been hit by a car."

"Don't make me laugh now, Johnny, my lips are chapped."

"Mommy, Mommy, the power mower's just cut off my foot!"

"Well, stay outside until the stump stops bleeding. I just washed the floor."

"Mommy, Mommy, the baby just fell into the fire."

"Shut up and get the marshmallows."

_____

"Mommy, Mommy, why can't I kiss Grandma?"

"Shut up and close the casket."

_____

"Mommy, Mommy, why can't we get a garbage disposal?"

"Shut up and keep chewing."

_____

"Mommy, Mommy, what happened to the baby's arm and legs?"

"Shut up and eat your drumsticks."

_____

"Mommy, Mommy, it's dark and wet down here."

"Shut up or I'll flush again."

"Mommy, Mommy, I don't want hamburger for dinner again."

"Be quiet and stick your arm back in the meat grinder."

"Mommy, Mommy, why can't I have a new puppy?"

"We haven't finished eating the old one yet."

"Mommy, Mommy, I don't want to go to Korea."

"Shut up and get in the CARE package."

"Mommy, Mommy, I want to go out and play baseball."

"You know you can't hold a bat with your hooks."

"Mommy, Mommy, why can't I go out and play in the snow?"

"You know your iron lung will rust."

"Mommy, Mommy, I can't feel my hand."

"Shut up or I'll cut your arm off, too."

"Mommy, Mommy, my tongue is sore."

"You've got to lick the bowl clean before I flush."

"Mommy, Mommy, Daddy's breathing again."

"Shut up and tighten the plastic bag around his neck."

"Mommy, Mommy, Daddy's up on his feet again."

"Be quiet and reload."

"Mommy, Mommy, I can't keep my mouth open any longer."

"Shut up. Your sister's almost finished shitting."

A man was looking for a grill in a department store. "What's the biggest rotisserie you have?" he asked the salesman. "I'm buying one for my sister and I want a big one. She's got five kids."

"This is the biggest one we have," the salesman said, pointing.

"No," the man said, shaking his head, "I doubt whether she could get more than three of the kids in there."

———————

"How did you get along with your new daddy while I was away?"

"Fine, Mommy. Every morning he took me on the lake in the rowboat and let me swim back."

"Wasn't that far to swim?"

"It was okay. The hard part was getting out of the bag first."

———————

"Joey, where's your sister?"

"She's out in the garage hanging herself from a beam."

"Go cut her down."

"She's not done yet."

———————

"Johnny, quit kicking your sister."

"That's all right, she's already dead."

"Dear, I think the children got into the rat poison."

"That's okay. They'll crawl under the house to die."

A boy was playing with his younger brother. "Could I fly like Superman?" the little tyke asked.

"Sure," his older brother replied. "Get up on the windowsill, flap your arms, and jump."

The little boy did as told. A few seconds later he smashed into the sidewalk eight stories below. The mother saw what happened from another room. She rushed in, horrified, and asked, "What happened?"

"I was teaching Junior not to believe everything people tell him."

"Mommy," the little boy said. "My turtle is dead."

The mother kissed him on the head, then said, "That's all right. We'll wrap it in tissue paper, put it in a box, then we'll have a burial ceremony in the backyard. Afterwards, we'll go out for an ice cream soda and then buy you a new pet. I don't want you to . . ." Her voice trailed off as she noticed the turtle move. "Jimmy, your turtle's not dead after all."

"Oh," the disappointed boy said. "Can I kill it?"

One man was explaining to another that he had a sure method for putting his baby to sleep. "I just toss it up in the air," he said.

"But why does that work?"

"We have very low ceilings."

———————————

What do you do with a dog that has no legs?

Take it out for a drag.

———————————

A woman and her eight-year-old daughter were walking in the fields one day when they saw a stallion mounting a mare. "Mommy," the little girl asked, "what are those horses doing in that field?"

The mother, embarrassed, hemmed and hawed a moment before she came up with an answer. "The horse on top hurt his hoof, and the one underneath is helping him back to the barn."

The little girl shook her head, then said, "That's the way it is with people, too. You try to help somebody and you get fucked."

———————————

"Mrs. Hilliard, can Herman come out and play?"

"Boys, you know Herman has no arms and legs."

"Yes. But we're playing hockey and we want to use him as the puck."

"Mrs. Fredericks, can the twins come out and play?"

"Johnny, you know they're in wheelchairs."

"Yes, but we want to roll them down Collins Hill and see which goes over the cliff first."

Eight-year-old Freddy and six-year-old Mindy were hiding in their big sister's closet as she entertained her boyfriend. They heard much panting and moaning before their sister sighed, "Oh, John, you're in where no man's been before."

Freddy turned to Mindy and said, "Wow. He must be fucking her in the ass!"

Chapter Four:

VULGAR CRIPPLE JOKES

A young woman received a call from a guy who said he'd seen her on the street. After a little persuasion, she agreed to go out with him. But when he arrived at her door, she was surprised to see that he had no arms and legs.

"I won't go out with you," she said. "What can you do for me?"

The cripple licked his lips and replied, "I dialed the telephone, didn't I?"

A man walked into his favorite watering hole and bought a round for the house. The bartender asked him why he looked so happy.

"I'm finally taller than my brother," the man said.

The bartender looked at him incredulously. "I can't believe you grew at your age?"

"I didn't. He was in an accident and they cut his legs off."

The beggar with no legs propelled his trolley by holding onto the tail of his dog. He was going down Main Street one day when a very stern looking woman came up to him and said, "I'm a member of the Society for the Prevention of Cruelty to Animals. Can't you find a better way to get around than holding onto that poor animal's tail?"

"Yeah," the beggar said. "I can grab his balls and go into high gear."

———————

A beautiful model married a man paralyzed from the neck down. A surprised girlfriend who knew the model loved sex asked her how the hell she could have made that choice.

"You don't understand," the model said. "John's got an eight-inch tongue."

"An eight-inch tongue?"

"And even better, he's learned to breathe through his ears."

A man was out for a walk when another man came bolting out of his front door, shouting, "My wife is having a seizure. My wife is having a seizure."

Being a good samaritan, the man dashed back inside with the husband. They raced up the stairs, where the wife, completely nude, was thrashing and jerking on the bed.

The husband tossed the man a rope and shouted, "Let's tie down her right leg." After a struggle, they secured that limb. Then they tied the left leg, and finally the two arms.

The husband thanked his benefactor, who turned to leave. "Wait, please," the husband said. To the man's amazement, he quickly stripped off his clothes, mounted his wife, and shouted, "Now cut her loose!"

Tom met a woman on the boardwalk sitting in a wheelchair. After a few minutes of conversation, he discovered that she was a paraplegic. But he found himself really attracted to her and sympathetic to her social problem.

The next night he presented himself at her door. He told her father he wanted to take her out. He helped her into his car and they went to a drive-in. Halfway through the second feature, he leaned over and kissed her. She responded passionately.

"What do you want to do afterwards?" he asked.

"I'd like to fuck," she said.

When the movie was over, she directed him to a country road. When they got out in the wilderness, she told him to stop and carry her toward the woods. They reached a tree with a horizontal branch. He laid her over the branch, fucked her, then put her in the car.

When they got home, the father was waiting up. Tom was overcome with guilt and he confessed, "I fucked your daughter tonight."

"That's okay, son," the father said. "All the other fellows have left her hanging over that branch."

A man called his friend in the middle of the night and said, "Fred, I'm really worried about Mary. She wasn't here when I got home from work and I still haven't heard from her. And you know how depressed she gets at times since her mastectomy."

Fred tried to reassure him. "Maybe she's just visiting a friend."

"I doubt it," the man said glumly. "She left her tits here."

———————

The wife came into her huband's study and said, "William, I want to tell you it's our mongoloid son's seventh birthday today. I think you should do something appropriate."

The man put down his paper and thought for a moment. "Okay," he said, "have the nurse wheel him in here."

A few minutes later, his son was sitting before him. He studied his offspring for a second, then began, "I think it's time we finally had a man to thing chat."

———————

One midget ran into another and asked, "How was your vacation at the nude ranch?"

"Strange. At first I thought I'd been hijacked to Havana. From my angle everybody looked like Fidel Castro."

How do you circumcise a leper?

Shake him.

A hump-backed American girl went to Paris, where she met a handsome French nobleman. The Frenchman soon proposed marriage, and the girl was in seventh heaven. All that remained before she marched down the aisle was to meet his mother, whose consent was necessary. As they entered her house on the appointed day, he told her there was nothing to worry about. "Just one thing, dear," he added. "You've got to straighten up."

The armless man was eating in the restaurant when he felt a strong call of nature. He persuaded the manager to take him into the restroom. "Take me into the stall and pull my pants down," the armless man instructed, "then wait outside."

The restaurant manager complied. A couple of minutes later, the armless man called out, "Did you hear a splash?"

"No."

"God dammit," the armless man complained, "you forgot to pull my shorts down."

What did the mean man do after he raped Helen Keller?

He cut off her hands so she couldn't yell for help.

_____

Why was Helen Keller's leg yellow?

Because her dog was blind, too.

_____

Why didn't Helen Keller make noise when she fell down the stairs?

She was wearing gloves.

_____

What was Helen Keller's speech impediment?

Calluses.

_____

How did Helen Keller's teacher punish her for talking in class?

She made her wear mittens.

Why didn't Helen Keller ever change her baby's diaper?

So she could always find him.

———————————

Why did Helen Keller masturbate with one hand?

So she could moan with the other.

———————————

Why didn't Helen Keller's bicycle have a front wheel?

So she could feel the road.

———————————

What's the cruelest present Helen Keller ever got?

Rubik's Cube.

———————————

What's the second cruelest present Helen Keller ever got?

A paint by number set.

What's the cruelest present Helen Keller ever gave?

Her first paint by number picture.

How did the speech therapist make Helen Keller's voice stronger?

He gave her a hand squeezer.

What did Helen Keller consider oral sex?

A manicure.

How did Helen Keller burn her face?

Answering the iron.

Why did the wheelchair basketball player have to go to the sports medicine specialist?

He came down with a bad case of athlete's stump.

What do a hemophiliac and a virgin have in common?

One prick and it's all over.

———————————

Two guys passed a female midget on the street. One said to the other, "I wonder what it's like having sex with a midget."

The other said, "I went out with a sex-crazed dwarf for a while."

"Really? What was it like?"

"Great. She always wanted to go up on me."

———————————

Why do farts smell?

So deaf people can enjoy them, too.

The new director was making a tour of the mental hospital. He rounded a corner and came upon a patient practicing a baseball swing without a bat. The director introduced himself, then asked, "Do you think you'll get out of here soon?"

"Sure," the patient said, "as soon as I hit this home run."

In another corridor, the director came upon a man swinging an imaginary golf club. In reply to the director's question, the man said, "I'll be out of here as soon as I make this hole in one."

Entering a third wing of the building, the director saw a man sitting on the floor with his pants down. A peanut was jammed on the end of his dick.

The director was surprised, but he asked, "Do you think you'll get out of here soon?"

The patient flashed him an annoyed look. "Are you kidding? I'm fucking nuts."

Chapter Five:

CANNIBAL JOKES

What do cannibals call unborn babies?

Hors d'oeuvres.

_____

What's the special at cannibal fast-food restaurants?

An all-beef missionary, special sauce, lettuce, cheese, onions, on a sesame bun.

The cannibals captured a seventy-year-old missionary. Since the old bird was so tough, they decided to cook him slowly over a low flame. The head cannibal put him in a pot of water, then came out for a taste two hours later. When the liquid touched his lips, a look of revulsion came over his face. He flung the liquid away and ordered the missionary taken into the forest and buried alive.

His number two man came up to him and said, "Chief, why throw good food away?"

The chief spat on the ground and said, "That bastard. He had the balls to piss in the pot."

———————

The cannibals had stripped the gorgeous blonde and were about to put her in the pot when the chief stopped them.

"Bring her into my hut," the chief said. "I think I'll have breakfast in bed."

———————

One cannibal turned to his dinner companion and said, "You know, I really hate my mother-in-law."

"Well, then," the other replied, "just eat the vegetables."

———————

What's the cannibal's favorite religious text?

How To Serve Your Fellow Man.

If civilized people can be vegetarians, why can't cannibals be humanitarians?

———————

A cannibal visited a neighbor to admire his new refrigerator.

"What's its storage capacity?" the man asked.

"I'm not exactly sure," the neighbor replied. "But it at least holds the two men who brought it."

———————

Two cannibal women were discussing marital problems. "I don't know what to make of my husband these days," one said.

The other said soothingly, "Don't worry, dear. I'll send over my recipe file."

———————

What social gaffe did the cannibal commit?

Trying to talk with someone's foot in his mouth.

———————

A cannibal went to the local witch doctor complaining that he was bored and depressed.

"The problem with you," the witch doctor said, "is that you're fed up with people."

A group of cannibals was walking along when an airplane flew by, far overhead. A child turned to his father and asked, "What's that?"

"It's something like a clam," the man explained. "It's got a hard shell and you only eat what's inside."

A newly arrived missionary asked the cannibal chief, "Do you know anything about Christianity?"

"Well," replied the chief, "we got a little taste of it when the last missionary was here."

A cannibal chief treated himself to a cruise. On the first night, he sat down at a table, asked for the wine list, and consumed nearly a bottle of a fine bordeaux. The waiter approached and asked if he'd like to see the menu.

"No," the chief replied. "Just bring me the passenger list."

"Shall I boil the new missionary?" the cannibal asked.

"God, no," the head man replied. "He's a friar."

The cannibal tribe caught and ate an American family that had been on safari. The next day, one of the cannibal boys was rummaging through their belongings when he found a copy of *Playboy*. He was tearing out the pictures of naked women and stuffing them into his mouth when a friend came in.

"Say," the friend asked, "is that dehydrated stuff any good?"

————————————

A missionary was surprised to find out that the cannibal chief had gone to school in England and spoke perfect English.

"I can't understand how you could have spent so much time in civilization and still eat people."

"But now I use a knife and fork."

————————————

Two cannibals, a father and son, were out hunting when they spotted a beautiful young girl bathing in a jungle stream.

"There's breakfast," the youngster said.

"She's too beautiful to eat," his father said.

"But I'm starved."

"Listen," the father explained. "We'll sneak up and capture her. Then we'll take her home and eat your mother for breakfast."

A trader leading a group of bearers carrying a load of bananas was captured by cannibals. Before they cooked him, the cannibals started shoving the bananas up the trader's ass. To their surprise, the trader started laughing hysterically.

"What's so funny?" the chief asked.

"My partner's a half day behind me," the trader said, "with a load of pineapples."

———————————

What do cannibals eat when they go on a diet?

Pygmies.

———————————

Word came back to the cannibal tribe that a group of politicians had been captured.

"Good," the chief commented. "I've always wanted to try a baloney sandwich."

Chapter Six:

MORTIFYING MEDICAL JOKES

The man waited anxiously in the doctor's office for over a half hour. Finally, the physician came in and told the man he had good news and bad news.

"Give me the bad news first," the man said.

"The bad news is that you have leukemia. You've only got three months to live."

"That's terrible!" the man exclaimed. He took a moment to collect his thoughts, then asked, "What's the good news?"

The doctor replied, "I've just fucked your wife, and I think we'll be very happy together after you've gone."

While doing a vasectomy, the doctor slipped and cut off one of the man's balls. To avoid a huge malpractice suit, he decided to replace the missing ball with an onion.

Several weeks later, the patient returned for a checkup.

"How's your sex life?" the doctor asked.

"Pretty good," the man said, to the doctor's relief. But then he added, "I've had some strange side effects."

"What's that?" the doctor asked anxiously.

"Well, every time I piss my eyes water. When my wife gives me a blow job she gets heartburn. And every time I pass a hamburger stand I get a hard-on."

John's tennis elbow had been killing him, so when he was passing by the doctor's office one day, he decided to stop in. The nurse told him he could see the doctor in twenty minutes, but first he had to provide a urine sample. John told her that was absurd for an elbow examination, but she insisted. Finally, he agreed.

Later, he was ushered in to see the doctor, who said, "That tennis elbow is really acting up, huh?"

"The nurse told you, then?" John asked.

"No," the doctor replied. "It's the urinalysis." He explained that he'd purchased a new machine that could diagnose absolutely every physical condition with total accuracy. The machine cost a fortune, but it cut down on his work so much that he was able to get out on the golf course at three every afternoon.

John didn't believe a word. However, he did agree to provide another urine sample when he came back in for another checkup.

Two weeks later, John was sitting at the breakfast table talking with his wife about the ridiculous machine. They decided to have some fun with the doctor. John pissed in the bottle, and so did his wife and teenage daughter. Then, as he opened the garage door, John had another idea. He put a few drops of crankcase oil from his car in the bottle, then beat off and added a few drops of semen. Then he shook up the bottle, drove to the doctor and handed the bottle to the nurse.

This time the analysis took a half-hour. When John sat down, the doctor looked at him and said, "All right, wise guy. I've got some bad news for you. Your daughter's pregnant, your wife's got V.D., your car is about to throw a rod, and if you don't stop beating off, that tennis elbow is never going to heal."

The doctor wanted to write a prescription, so he reached in his pocket and pulled out a thermometer. "Shit," he muttered, "some asshole has my pen."

A woman went to her doctor for a physical examination. The doctor found out she was in perfect health, but he couldn't figure something out. He asked her what possible reason she could have for having wax in her belly button.

"My husband likes to eat by candlelight," she said.

The lady wasn't feeling good, so she went to the doctor. He examined her all over, and kept saying, "Ah hah." He put his finger up her rear and said, "Ah hah." Then he put his finger in her mouth and said, "Ah hah." Finally the woman asked the doctor what she had.

The doctor said, "I hate to tell you, but you have exacalees."

"What's that?" the surprised woman asked.

"Well, you got a rotten smell in your ass, and that's exacalees the same smell you got in your mouth."

What happened to the woman who swallowed the razor blade?

In a week, she gave herself a hysterectomy, castrated her husband, circumcised her lover, took two fingers off a friend, and gave her minister a hairlip.

The man woke up in the hospital after the terrible car crash. His doctor was at his bedside, and the man asked anxiously, "What happened to me?"

"Well," the doctor said, "I've got some bad news and some good news. The bad news is that both of your legs are gone."

"My God!" the man cried. "What could possibly be good after that?"

"The good news is that those pesky corns of yours are completely gone."

A construction worker was rushed to the hospital after cutting himself badly. The doctor told the nurse to prepare a pain killer so he could stitch the wound.

"Don't bother, Doc," the guy said, "I've been through a lot worse."

"More painful than this?" the doctor asked.

"I'll tell you about the second most painful accident I had. I was hunting one day and I had to take a dump, so I dropped my pants and squatted. I tripped a bear trap and boom, the thing snapped shut on my balls."

The doctor winced. "That's awful. But tell me, what could be worse?"

"When I pulled the end of the chain."

A teenager went to the doctor complaining of a dripping cock. The doctor took a look and told him he had V.D.

"That's impossible," the teenager cried. "It must be a cold."

"Maybe," said the physician. "But we have to treat it like V.D. until it sneezes."

What's the difference between herpes and true love?

Herpes lasts forever.

A guy met a gorgeous woman in a bar who confessed that she had an incredible foot fetish. The guy said what the hell, went home with her, and fucked her with his big toe.

A few days later the toe began to swell. He went to the doctor, who told him he had syphilis of the foot.

"Is that unusual?" the guy asked.

"No," the doctor replied. "I had a lady in here earlier who had athlete's cunt."

The intern stopped in a sleezy downtown coffee shop, the only place open at 3 A.M. The waitress who came over was scratching her ass as she waited for him to make up his mind.

"Do you have hemorrhoids?" the intern asked.

"No special orders," the waitress barked.

The absent-minded surgeon walked out of the operating room. A colleague came running up to him and said, "George, how did that appendectomy on my wife go?"

"Appendectomy?" George replied. "I just did an autopsy."

The Hell's Angel took his nymphomaniac girlfriend to the doctor to find out if she was pregnant. In the examining room, the doctor's first touch was enough to send the girl writhing and moaning. The sight was too much to resist, and the doctor climbed on. He was so caught up in the passion he didn't realize how loud she was until the door slammed open and the huge, mean-looking biker stormed in.

"What in the hell do you think you're doing, Doc?" the Hell's Angel demanded.

"Uh, uh, taking her temperature," the doctor stammered.

The biker reached into his belt, took out a switchblade, and flicked the knife open. "Well, Doc, if that thermometer doesn't have numbers on it when it comes out, it's coming off."

———————————

A man called his doctor and told him he had a problem with his wife. "She has a bowel movement at seven o'clock every morning."

"That's perfectly normal," the doctor said.

"But we don't get out of bed until nine."

The woman went to the clinic for artificial insemination. The doctor had her place her feet in the stirrups, then he started to undo his pants.

"Wait a minute," the woman said. "What are you doing?"

"I'm out of the bottled stuff," the doctor replied. "You'll have to settle for what's on tap."

———————

A man woke up after an appendectomy with a huge bandage over his groin as well as one over his abdomen. He rang the bell, and eventually the doctor came in.

"What in the hell is that bandage for?" the man asked anxiously.

"I've got to apologize for that," the surgeon said. "The appendectomy was such a success that the medical students applauded. When I bowed I cut off your prick with the scalpel."

———————

A man charged into the druggist's office, shouting, "You gave my wife cyanide instead of a bromide!"

"That's terrible," the druggist said. "You owe me another ten dollars."

70

"Boy, I got tired of the interruptions when I was in the hospital," a man said to his friend.

"Nurses coming in all the time, huh?"

"Yeah. It got so when someone knocked at the door I called out 'Friend or enema?'"

———————

Why did the dentist spend his entire vacation in a whorehouse?

He wanted bigger cavities to drill.

———————

The woman called her psychiatrist and said, "I'm terribly worried about my son. We've just caught him with the four-year-old girl next door, examining each other with their pants down."

"Don't worry, Mrs. Jones," the shrink said. "It's natural for children to have curiosity."

"Well, I'm very worried, Doctor," the woman said. "And so's my son's wife."

A backwoodsman walked into a surgeon's office and announced, "Doc, I want you to castrate me."

"What?" the doctor asked. "A big, husky fellow like you?"

"No questions," the man said firmly. "Just castrate me. Here's your money."

Shrugging his shoulders, the doctor called his nurse in. She administered the ether, and the patient lost the power of his sex. As he came to, the doctor leaned over and asked, "While you're on the table, do you want to be circumcised?"

"Dawgone it, Doc," the patient said in a high-pitched voice, "that's the word I wanted. That's what I wanted done!"

A man called the dentist's office and said, "Doc, I've got an emergency. While my wife and I were out, my son was kissing his girlfriend and got his braces locked."

"No problem," the dentist said, "I have to unlock teenager's braces all the time."

"From an I.U.D.?"

A man rushed into the dentist's office and insisted the dental assistant leave the room. When she was gone, he unzipped his fly and pulled out his prick.

"Wait a second," the dentist said. "I don't treat V.D."

"It isn't V.D.," the man said. "I've got a tooth embedded in it."

Two hippies were so opposed to the idea of going to Viet Nam that they had all their teeth pulled out, so the Army wouldn't take them.

They showed up at 6 A.M. at the Army Induction Center for their physical and got in line to see the medic. Unfortunately, a big farmer who smelled like he hadn't bathed in a year got between them, and the stench made the hour wait seem like two. Finally the first hippie got to the medic and told him he had no teeth. The medic looked in his mouth and said, "Okay, you're 4F."

Next came the big farmer. "What's wrong with you?" the medic asked.

"I got real bad piles," the farmer said.

The medic stuck a finger up the farmer's ass, then said, "All right, you're 4F."

The second hippie came up and stared at the shitty, foul-smelling finger of the medic.

"Well," the medic said, "what's wrong with you?"

"Nothing," the hippie said. "Absolutely nothing."

A woman was sitting in the doctor's office when he came in and said, "Mrs. Jones, this isn't a urine sample you brought in. It's apple juice."

"Oh my God," she said. "I've got to get to a phone."

"Why?"

"I must have packed the other bottle in Jimmy's lunch box."

Chapter Seven:

INDECENT RELIGIOUS JOKES

What kind of meat do priests eat on Friday?

Nun.

The Mother Superior was sitting at her desk as the little girls in the school came up to tell her what they wanted to be when they grew up. The first group of twenty all said they wanted to be nuns. Another group of twenty came in and all said the same thing. Mother Superior was growing tired as the first girl of the third group approached and announced she wanted to become a prostitute.

"What?" the outraged nun screamed, leaping to her feet.

The girl repeated that she wanted to become a prostitute.

The Mother Superior breathed a loud sigh of relief. "Oh, that's all right," she said. "I thought you said you wanted to become a Protestant."

The old priest and the nun were on their way to a desert mission by camel when they became lost. Four days later the camel dropped dead, and the two were about to abandon all hope. Before dying, the priest desperately wanted to fuck a woman, so he pulled out his cock and showed it to the nun. "Sister," he asked, "do you know what this is?"

"No, I don't."

"It's the staff of life," the priest told her.

"Thank God!" she exclaimed. "Then stick it up that camel's ass and let's ride out of here."

Two veteran whores decided they'd had enough of street life and they joined the Salvation Army. They stayed for three months, then Wanda changed her mind. She told Mary that she had to have another trick and get herself a bottle. Later that night Mary was holding a street service when Wanda came staggering by. "Friends," Mary was preaching, "I used to be in the arms of sailors; I used to be in the arms of soldiers; I used to be in the arms of Marines. But now I'm in the arms of the Lord."

Wanda shouted, "Way to go, Mary. Fuck them all."

A priest was hearing the confession of a little girl when he heard a drunk stumble noisily into the booth on the other side. After absolving the child of her sins, the priest turned and opened the little panel to the other booth.

"Are you all right?" he asked.

All he heard was a long grunt.

"Are you all right?" he asked again.

Finally, the drunk replied, "Yeah, I feel a lot better. But do you have any toilet paper over on your side?"

————————————

A young Catholic girl confessed that she'd masturbated her boyfriend the night before. The priest ordered her to repeat ten Hail Marys and ten Our Fathers while washing her hands in the holy water basin.

The girl was almost finished when her girlfriend approached and asked what she was doing. She replied, "I jerked off Joe last night and this is my penance."

"Don't get the water too dirty," her friend said. "I'll probably have to gargle with it."

Christ was hanging on the cross when he yelled out, "John! John!" From amidst the crowd John bolted toward the cross. A Roman soldier saw him and, with one swipe of his sword, cut off the apostle's legs.

A few minutes later, Christ called out again, "John! John!" Using only his arms, John pulled himself toward his savior. Another soldier saw him, cut off his arms, and threw him back into the crowd.

Once again Christ cried, "John! John!"

Again from the crowd John responded, this time pulling himself by his chin. After an incredible effort, the apostle got to the base of the cross and gasped, "Here I am, my Lord. What do you want?"

Christ looked down and said, "John, from up here I can see your house."

––––––––––––

What did Christ say while he was hanging on the cross?

"What a hell of a way to spend my Easter vacation."

––––––––––––

The three nuns were walking across the street, discussing their vacations. One held up her hands to show the tremendous-sized pineapples she'd seen in Hawaii.

The second nun stretched her hands out to show how big the bananas were in Haiti.

The third nun, a trifle deaf, asked, "Father who?"

Chapter Eight:

FOUL HOMOSEXUAL JOKES

Two homosexuals met in a gay bar, fell in love, and decided to move in together. After a weekend of bliss, one got up on Monday morning and went into the bathroom to shower and shave to go to work. When he emerged, he found his lover in the kitchen masturbating into a baggie.

"What are you doing, honey?" he asked.

"Packing your lunch."

———————————

What do you call a homosexual who likes to screw men with hemorrhoids?

A pile driver.

———————————

One fag was fucking another in the pitch-black back room of a gay bar. When he finished, he rolled off and said, "That was great. Was that one of those fancy ribbed condoms you gave me?"

"No," the other fag said. "I've got hemorrhoids."

What did one lesbian say to the other?

"Your face or mine?"

_____

Did you hear about the male prostitute who got leprosy?

He did okay until his business fell off.

_____

How can you tell a tough lesbian bar?

Even the pool table doesn't have any balls.

_____

Why are male prostitutes like Inspector Clouseau?

They're both Peter Sellers.

_____

What do gays eat for dinner?

Semen Helper.

What is Polish lesbians' favorite food?

Smelt.

––––––––––––––––

Why don't they hire homosexuals at the sperm bank?

Too many get caught drinking on the job.

––––––––––––––––

What did the lesbian gas station attendant say to the leggy blonde who drove in?

"Mind if I check under your hood?"

––––––––––––––––

The fag went to church and when they passed the collection basket, he dropped $50 in. When the minister saw this, he asked him to stand up. The minister said that in honor of his generous contribution he could take his choice of three hymns. The fag stood, turned toward the congregation, then lisped, "Okay, I'll take him, and him, and him."

Two homosexuals were out riding in a car. The passenger started caressing the driver, who was so distracted he smashed into a delivery truck. The burly truck driver raced up and started screaming and arguing, finally shouting, "Kiss my ass!"

The homosexual took a step back and said, "Now you stop that. This is no time to make love."

———————————

A wild weekend in the back rooms of gay bars left Ronny with an incredibly swollen, sore rectum. Unable to sleep, he called a friend who told him to shove a couple of handfuls of herbal tea up his ass. The advice seemed to help a bit.

The next morning, though, Ronny hurried to the gay proctologist's office. The doctor had him spread his cheeks and started exploring.

"What's wrong with me?" Ronny asked after a couple minutes.

"I don't know exactly, darling," the fag doctor replied, "but the tea leaves say you and I should take a long sea cruise together."

Two women were walking down the street when they saw two homosexuals kissing passionately. "Ugh," one said to the other, "that's disgusting. They ought to ship every one of those queers to some island, so we wouldn't have to look at them."

"They can't do that," the other woman said. "We'd all have to cut our own hair and decorate our own apartments."

———————————

Why is there so little fraternizing on naval ships?

Because the sailors seldom see each other face to face.

———————————

For appearances' sake, the gay businessman got married. When he returned from his honeymoon, one of his macho colleagues slapped him on the back and asked jovially, "Did you knock up the bride?"

"God, I hope so," the closet queen exclaimed. "I don't think I could go through that again."

———————————

What's a gay masochist?

A sucker for punishment.

Why didn't the lesbian tennis star compete in the Dutch Open?

She got her finger stuck in a dyke.

The flaming fag was walking by the construction sight when he saw a gorgeous he-man. He stopped, gawked, then began flirting outrageously. Finally, the construction worker shouted, "Get out of here, you queer, or I'll ram this jackhammer up your ass."

"Ooooo," twitted the fag as he bent over. "I thought you'd never ask."

What happened to the fat, ugly gay guy?

He had to go out with girls.

Why did the parents have their child christened in Greenwich Village?

So he could have a fairy godfather.

What do they call sex-change operations?

Artificial infemination.

What's the difference between a priest and a homo-sexual?

The way they pronounce A-men.

Three men armed with shotguns stormed into a late-night diner in Greenwich Village. "Everybody down on the floor!" one shouted. "We're going to rape all the men and rob all the women."

"No," another said. "That's wrong. We're going to rob all the men and rape all the women."

At that a fag in the corner piped up, "I think you should listen to that first darling."

Did you hear about the transvestite who had two tits grafted onto his back?

If his ass holds out, he'll be a millionaire.

The police department received a call at 1 A.M. from a professor at the local university who reported a break-in. "The man was a huge brute," the professor reported. "He ripped the covers off the bed and found me sleeping naked. He looked at me in the most vile possible way and then he exposed this incredibly large penis."

"That sounds awful," the sympathetic police clerk responded.

"That's not the worst part. He made me put that disgusting thing in my mouth, then he turned me over and shoved it up my ass until I felt like I would split in two. Then he pissed all over me."

"We'll send a squad over right away to look for him," the clerk said.

"Oh, you don't have to do that," the professor said. "He's in the shower now. Why don't you just come over and pick him up in the morning."

What did the lesbian say as she guided her girlfriend's tongue to her clitoris?

"This bud's for you."

What do they call a bouncer in a gay bar?

A flame thrower.

What kind of vibrator do really macho butch lesbians use?

Ones with a kick starter.

———————————

A compulsive gambler walked into a gay bar. He sat down between a couple of fags, ordered a drink, and struck up a conversation with one. When that guy went to the john, the gambler turned to the fag on his left and bet him $50 he had hemorrhoids. The fag had just been to the doctor for a rectal examination and knew he had no hemorrhoids, so he agreed to the bet. He got up and dropped his drawers. When he bent over, the gambler shoved a broomstick up his ass and sure enough, found no hemorrhoids. He paid the fag $50 bucks and headed for the rest room.

The delighted winner sat back down on his stool. When the other fag came back to the bar, the guy told him he'd won $50.

"How?"

"He bet me I had hemorrhoids. I knew I didn't so I dropped my drawers. When I did, he shoved a broomstick up my ass."

A look of shock came on the other fag's face. "That son-of-a-bitch. A few minutes ago he bet me $100 he'd have a broomstick shoved up your ass in 15 minutes!"

On the first day out to sea, the new crew member noticed his shipmates were a rough lot. After every meal, the men would belch and fart incredibly noisily, like cannons firing.

The second day he decided to join his mates and he ventured a gentle "Phtt." Suddenly, the second mate, a towering giant, rose up, slammed his fist on the table and announced, "All right, men. The virgin is mine!"

––––––––––––––––

The man walked into the sperm bank and up to the woman at the desk. "Can I help you?" she asked.

The man nodded his head.

"Well?"

The man made some gestures she didn't understand.

"You'll have to tell me what you want," she said impatiently. "Can't you talk?"

He shook his head no.

"Well," she said, "I guess you want to deposit some sperm. Right? Just take a bottle and go into one of the booths."

The man shook his head no. Finally, she pulled out a pad and a pencil and said, "You'll have to write down what you want."

The man took the pencil and wrote, "I don't have to go into the room. I've got the sperm in my mouth."

Two homosexuals passed on the street. One stopped the other and exclaimed, "Darling, I thought they'd sent you to jail on that sodomy charge?"

"Oh, no," the other exclaimed. "I found this wonderful lawyer who got the charge reduced to 'following too closely.'"

———————

A transvestite was out cruising the street when he was approached by a huge, rough-looking Polack. As usual, the transvestite told the guy that he was having his period and could only give blowjobs. The Pole told him he wanted to fuck him in the ass instead. The guy was so mean looking that the transvestite agreed. Soon there was a big cock buried in his ass and the transvestite started to get a hard-on in his excitement. The Polack put his hand around to the front, felt the stiff prick, and exclaimed, "Hot damn. In one end and out the other!"

Chapter Nine:

LEWD SENIOR CITIZEN JOKES

An eighty-four-year-old man hobbled into the whorehouse and told the madam that he had to have a girl with gonorrhea. The madam tried to talk him out of it, but the stubborn old coot wouldn't hear of anything else. Finally, the madam took one of her girls aside and said, "Lucy, tell the old geezer you've got gonorrhea and give him a little fun."

She went up to him, whispered in his ear, and took him upstairs. The old man was surprisingly frisky in bed. Afterwards, Lucy felt guilty about her deception. "I've got a confession," she said. "I really don't have gonorrhea."

"Now you do," the old man said.

———————————

How can you tell an old man in the dark?

It's not hard.

What did one old maid say to the other?

"Let's go down to the cucumber patch and do push-ups."

———————

What was in the old maid's heart-shaped locket?

A picture of a candle.

———————

"Did you hear what happened to old Miss Johnson?"
"No."
"She died from using a vibrator."
"She couldn't take the strain of sex at her age?"
"Nope. The battery short-circuited her pacemaker."

———————

The word spread like wildfire at the country club that the seventy-year-old industrialist had married a twenty-year-old chorus girl. One of the other members finally asked him how he'd talked her into it.

"I told her I was ninety," he replied.

———————

What's the most useless thing in Grandma's house?

Grandpa's thing.

Two old women were sitting on a park bench, enjoying the sunshine. One turned to the other and said, "I hate being old. My husband is so stubborn he won't have sex any other way but doggie-style."

"Don't complain," the other woman said. "My husband can only have sex coyote-style—lie beside the hole and howl."

———————

The old codger hobbled into the doctor's office. "You here for a checkup, grandpa?" the doctor asked.

"Nope," the old man replied. "My wife caught me in bed with a whore and she sent me down to make sure I didn't catch nothing."

"That's smart," the doctor said. "Now, let me see your sex organ."

The old man held up his index finger.

———————

Grandpa and Grandma were babysitting for their five-year-old grandson. They were in the living room watching television when they heard a noise from the kitchen. Grandpa, who was pretty spry, got there in a hurry. He found that the kid had swallowed some kitchen cleaner stored under the sink.

His shriveled old wife hobbled in, saw the boy writhing on the floor, and asked, "What should we do?"

"We've got to make him vomit," the old man said. "Quick, lift up your skirt and show him your cunt."

A guy picked up an older woman in a bar and took her back to his place for an evening of fucking. As the grinding and groaning picked up tempo, he let his lips stray to the woman's sagging tit. Latching firmly onto the nipple, he began to suck vigorously—and got a mouthful of liquid.

"Jesus," he exclaimed, "aren't you too old to be giving milk?"

"Yes, honey," she replied. "But I'm not too old to have cancer."

An eighty-five-year-old lady lived with her sixty-year-old son. One Mother's Day her son offered to fuck her as a present. She was grateful, but a couple of minutes after he entered, she shit all over herself.

The son rolled off and said, "Mother, what the hell are you doing?"

The old lady said, "Son, I'm too old to come, but you know I love you so much I had to do something."

An old man saved a few dollars from every pension check until he had enough money to hire a call girl. After much effort on her part, he managed to raise an erection but no matter how hard she worked, nothing else happened. A week after, however, the old man noticed a drip from his penis. Worried, he hurried to the doctor.

After running tests, the doctor asked, "Have you had sex lately?"

The old man said yes.

"Well," the doctor said, "do you know the woman well enough to get her over here right now?"

"I . . . I'm not sure I can afford it," the old man stammered.

"I think you ought to," the doctor said, "because you're finally ready to come."

———————————

The madam hung up the phone, turned around, and said, "April, it's the nursing home again."

"Damn," the whore spat. "I hate that call."

"Why? Those old guys pay twice the going rate for practically no work."

"The sex isn't the problem," the hooker replied. "I just hate changing their shitty diapers first."

The old man walked into the whorehouse and approached the madam. "I'd like to have sex with a young girl," he said.

She took one look at him and said, "You must be over ninety."

"92."

"Well, pop, I think you've had it."

The old man looked confused for a moment. Then he said, "I have? How much do I owe?"

_____

One guy said to another, "That woman I saw you with last night must have been well over sixty years old. What do you see in her?"

"I like women that age," his friend replied. "They don't swell, they don't tell, they don't smell, and they're grateful as hell."

Chapter Ten:

RAUNCHY SEX JOKES

Two women were attending the funeral of a friend who had been married eight times. One sighed and said, "They're together at last."

"Which husband are you talking about?" the other asked.

"None of her husbands. I mean her legs."

———————————

The dentist was surprised to see three broken teeth in the mouth of the gorgeous model. "What the hell happened to you?" he asked.

"I don't know," she said. "I was giving head to this reporter named Clark Kent, and bamm, his prick turned to iron."

A king had to go away on the crusades, but his wife was so beautiful that he wasn't sure he could trust his eleven young male servants. So he went to a blacksmith and asked him for the strongest chastity belt in the place. The man brought out a strong belt with a hole in the center. The king was skeptical until the blacksmith said, "Here, put this broomstick in the hole." The king complied, and the broomstick was chopped off. The monarch happily took the belt, put it on his wife, and headed off to the holy wars.

Ten years later he returned and lined up all his servants to inspect their private parts. Ten of them were now eunuchs. But the king was delighted to see that the eleventh was intact. He put his arm around this faithful follower and asked, "What can I do to thank you?"

"Ahahaghagha," the servant answered.

———————————

The voluptuous blonde's car broke down, and she hitched a ride from a man riding a bicycle. After several miles, she leaned back and said over her shoulder, "You're not very observant. You haven't noticed I'm not wearing anything beneath my dress."

"You're the one who's not observant," he replied. "You haven't noticed this is a girl's bicycle."

———————————

Why was the guard with the Oedipus complex fired from his job at the museum?

For fucking the mummies.

How do you recondition an old whore?

Shove a ten pound ham up her cunt and pull out the bone.

Why are just-deflowered virgins like the warships in Pearl Harbor after the Japanese bombing?

Because their cock-pits are full of bloody semen.

The two maiden English ladies were very concerned about the scandalous behavior of their butler, an old and valued servant whose sex drive had increased enormously. One day, after the butler had been caught screwing the young upstairs maid, the maiden ladies reluctantly warned the butler that he'd be dismissed if he didn't turn over a new leaf. But the next evening the butler was caught in the wine cellar buggering a young boy.

"How dare you engage in such a perversion?" one of the ladies asked.

"You told me to turn over a new leaf, madam," the butler replied. "I decided to start with the bottom of the page."

The wife coyly tried to explain her purchase of a new pair of expensive imported panties. "After all, dear," she said, "you wouldn't expect to find fine perfume in a cheap bottle, would you?"

"No," her husband replied. "Nor would I expect to find gift wrapping on a dead beaver."

The doctor asked the young man how the accident happened. He replied, "We were making love on the living room rug when the chandelier suddenly crashed down on us."

"You're lucky," the doctor said. "You only sustained minor lacerations of the buttocks."

"I'll say," the young man said. "A minute earlier and I would have had a fractured skull."

While sightseeing on an Indian reservation, the young man was approached by a gorgeous maiden who made a familiar proposition for $50.

"Well," the man said, "that's a lot of money. It only cost $24 for Manhattan Island."

The girl smiled. "But Manhattan just lays there."

The father was reading his newspaper when his daughter's boyfriend asked to speak with him.

"I realize this is only a formality," the young man said. "But I want to ask for your daughter's hand in marriage."

The father said sternly, "What makes you think this is a formality?"

"The rabbit that just died."

———————————

The shapely blonde walked into the bar wearing skintight pants with no buttons, no zippers, no lace, nothing.

After staring awhile, the guy at the bar next to her asked, "I've been wondering, lady. How do you get into your pants?"

She smiled and said, "You can start by ordering me a drink."

———————————

One day *Mr. Good-Bar* decided he
   needed a *Bit-O-Honey*
So he went to Miss *Hershey*
He took her behind the *Power House*
   where he felt her *Mounds*
   which were pure *Almond Joy*
She *Snicker*ed as he put his
   Butter Finger up her *Milky Way*
She screamed, *O Henry*, then she squeezed
   his *Nutty Buddy*
His *Bazooka* fired
   Results—*Baby Ruth*

What did Pinocchio say to the old carpenter?

"Quit bitching about your crabs. I've got termites."

Allan, Brian and Mike were captured by the Nazis. The Germans told them they would only let them go if their penis sizes totalled up to 12 inches. Allan walked in and he measured 6½ inches. Mike added 5 inches. Finally Brian walked in and he measured ½ inch. So the Nazis let them go, and Allan said, "If it wasn't for my 6½ inches, we would never have gotten out." Mike said, "Well, if it wasn't for my 5 inches, we'd still be prisoners." Brian challenged, "Oh, yeah? Well, if it wasn't for my hard-on we could have been dead."

Three traveling salesmen were put up in one bed by a mother and daughter. When the men went to bed, the mother and daughter put their ear up to the door to hear what they were saying. The first guy talked about the million dollars he was going to inherit. The mother said to the daughter, "That's the guy for you." Then they heard the second guy was going to inherit two million, and the mother said, "No, that's the man for you." Then they heard the third man say, "All right, roll off my prick and let me go to sleep."

"I'm not on your prick," the guy next to him said.

"Well if it's not you who's on it, it must be over you and Mike is on it."

The daughter turned to her mother with a gleam in her eye and announced, "That's the man for me!"

The bride and groom reached the honeymoon suite. She said to him, "Johnny, now that we're married, could you tell me what a penis is?"

Pleased that his wife was a virgin, he took out his penis and showed it to her.

"Oh," she said, "it's just like a prick, only littler."

The businessman came home from work about 6 P.M. He'd barely got in the door before his wife greeted him with a passionate kiss. Then she pulled him into the bedroom, pushed him down on the bed, unzipped his pants, and began to suck on his cock.

The man stared at her a moment, then grimaced. "All right, Mildred," he said, "what did you do to the car this time."

Two men were walking out of the porno movie theater. One said to the other, "Boy, I wish I was hung like that John Holmes. If I had twelve inches I'd have girls lined up around the block. Maybe I should try one of those penis enlargers they advertise in the magazines."

"Forget it," his friend said. "I ordered one six months ago."

"It didn't work?"

"My prick didn't grow a bit. But now I've got a two foot square wallet and a six foot long belt."

The car of a beautiful but not too bright blonde was pulled over by a highway patrolman. He asked to see her license and registration, but was more captivated by her cleavage. He handed her back her papers and started to unzip his pants.

"Oh, no," she said as his prick emerged. "Not another breathalyzer test!"

The middle-aged guy started out for the whorehouse, but wandered into a sewing-machine office by mistake. The girl at the front desk said to him, "Well, sir, what kind would you like?" The guy said, "It depends on the price." The girl said, "There are some for $50 and some for $100."

"Bullshit," said the guy. "Last time I was in here I paid $20."

"Oh," the girl said. "Them. They're the kind that don't have any legs. You have to screw them on the table."

"Shit," the guy responded. "I don't give a fuck about the table part, but I'll be damned if I screw one without legs."

Why did the man trade his wife for an outhouse?

The hole was tighter and it smelled better.

How can you tell a woman is pregnant with a boy?

If she's happy. A woman is always happy with a prick in her.

Fact: The average length of a penis is six inches.

Fact: The average vaginal capacity is eight inches.

Fact: In New York City there is over 200 miles of unused vagina.

What's the smallest cemetery in the world?

A woman's vagina—it only takes one stiff at a time.

Two newlyweds arrived at their hotel from the reception. The wife went into the bathroom to get into something more comfortable and emerged wearing only a towel. Her husband told her to drop the towel because he wanted to take a picture of her in the nude to carry with him all the time. She dropped the towel, he exclaimed at her gorgeous body, then he took his snapshot.

A few minutes later, he emerged from the bathroom with only a towel around him. She told him to drop the towel, which he did. She stared for a moment, then said she wanted to take a picture, too.

"To carry with you?" he asked.

"No," she said. "I want to have it enlarged."

———————————

Two newlyweds went to their hotel. But the bride was too embarrassed to take off her clothes. Her husband told her to go into the bathroom, undress, then run to him in the dark. When she called out that she was ready, he turned off the lights and went running toward her. The room was so black that they missed each other. He went flying out the window and landed in the bushes. He screamed and screamed for help, but it was nearly half an hour before someone called back that everybody was too busy inside the hotel watching the lady who was stuck on a doorknob.

A man came home and found his wife sliding down the bannister. He asked what she was doing.

"Warming up your dinner," she replied.

What's the difference between a man and a shower?

If you don't know, don't get under either one of them.

What's the best sanitary napkin for girls who go dancing?

Discotex.

Why should the Pilgrims have killed cats instead of turkeys?

Because every Thanksgiving we could eat pussy.

The doctor came into the office and announced to the man, "The tests show you've got gonorrhea."

The man jumped to his feet in a rage. He stormed out of the office and down to the corner, where a black hooker paraded her wares. He grabbed her and shouted, "You filthy bitch, you gave me the clap."

The whore pulled away from him and snapped, "You got it wrong, honky. I didn't *give* you the clap, you *bought* it."

———————————

The couple sat glumly in the marriage counselor's office. "This all started the morning after our honeymoon," the man said. "I was so groggy when I woke up that I laid a $20 bill on the pillow."

"Well, that's not so bad," the counselor said. "You were just recalling your bachelor days."

"I know that," the man snapped. "But then my bride opened her eyes and barked, 'You're $20 short needledick.'"

The very snobbish wife was discussing the subject of Christmas presents with her maid. "Now what about the butler?" the rich woman said.

"A set of wine glasses?" the maid suggested.

The woman frowned icily. "He doesn't really need that. A butler never entertains. He'll get a tie."

The maid grimaced, but said only, "What about a dress for Jenny, the serving girl?"

The woman frowned again. "She doesn't really need a new dress. She'll only get in trouble. We'll get her another apron."

The conversation continued in the same vein, and the maid was chafing at her employer's arrogance when they reached her husband.

"I assume you want to get him something he really needs, madam?" the maid asked.

"Of course," the woman replied.

"Then what about five more inches?"

————————————

A very naive WASP couple complained to the doctor that they'd been trying to have a baby for months.

"What position are you in when you ejaculate?" the physician asked the husband.

"What's ejaculation?" the man asked.

"Well, uh, that's your climax," the doctor said.

The young man looked puzzled for a moment. Then he asked, "Do you mean the white stuff? Well, Buffy says it's icky, so I shoot it in the sink before we start."

After attending a Mexican bullfight, an American tourist ate supper at a nearby cafe. While he was eating, he saw a fellow dining on two large, juicy meatballs. He called over the waiter, who explained the dish was called El Toro Cojones and came from the bull slain at the arena.

The next day the tourist returned to the cafe and ordered El Toro Cojones. However, when the dish was served, there were only two small, shriveled meatballs. "This isn't what I ordered," the tourist complained. "I want two large juicy ones like the guy ate last night."

The waiter shrugged. "I'm sorry, señor," he said. "The bull does not always lose."

A man became increasingly furious over his wife's frequent refusals of his sexual advances. They fought like cats and dogs so often that his wife was amazed when he arrived home one day carrying a huge, elaborately wrapped present.

"What's that?" she asked.

"Open it."

She undid the wrapping and found a box with six live kittens. "Why kittens?"

He replied, "Six pallbearers for that dead pussy of yours."

A trucker walked into a restaurant and ordered a bowl of chicken noodle soup. After receiving his order, he raised a huge fuss. The owner came over and asked him what was wrong.

"There's a hair in my soup," the trucker said angrily. "And I refuse to pay." He got up, stormed out the door, and walked across the street to a whorehouse.

The owner, anxious to get his money, followed. He pushed by the madam and into a room, where he saw the trucker eating out a whore. "You bastard," he shouted. "You wouldn't pay for your soup because it had one hair in it, and now look at you."

The trucker pulled his head up and replied, "And I'll tell you another thing. If I find a noodle in here, I ain't paying for that either."

A man went to a sex therapist to complain that his wife never climaxed at the same time he did. The therapist replied that he'd had a similar problem years before that he'd solved by putting a pistol under his pillow. When he was going to climax, he pulled out the gun, fired a shot, and his wife climaxed with him.

The man promised to try the solution. Late that night the therapist got a call that the man had been rushed to the hospital. When he entered the man's room, he asked, "What happened?"

The man, grimacing in pain, said, "I placed a .45 under the pillow like you said. My wife was in the mood, so we went to bed and started making out. Just as I was about to climax, I fired the gun."

"Then what happened?"

"She shit in my face and bit the end of my dick off."

A man met a cute young thing in a disco and hustled her out to the parking lot for a quickie in the back seat. Afterwards, while he pulled up his pants, he said, "Honey, if I'd known you were a virgin, I'd have taken a little more time."

She looked at him sourly and said, "Buster, if you hadn't been in such a hurry, I would have taken off my pantyhose."

A very attractive chick went into a bar one afternoon and ordered a bottle of Budweiser. After she drank it, she passed out. The bartender suggested to the only customer that they take her in the back room and fuck her, which they did.

Word got around, and the next day there were a dozen guys in the bar. She came in, ordered another Budweiser, drank it, and passed out. The dozen guys took her in the back room and fucked her.

On the third day, twenty-four studs were two-deep at the bar, and they all were satisfied when she drank the Budweiser and passed out. But on the fourth day, the woman came in and ordered a Coors.

Immediately, fifty guys groaned. The bartender said to her, "But you always drink Budweiser."

"I decided to change," she said. "Budweiser's starting to make my cunt hurt."

A hillbilly went to a whorehouse for the first time. The madam asked him if he had any experience. "No," he admitted.

"In this house, you have to have experience." She recommended he go home and fuck tree holes.

The next day he came back and claimed to have experience. She sent him upstairs. Suddenly there was a scream. She ran up and saw the hillbilly ramming a broomstick up the whore's cunt. When she asked him what he was doing, he replied, "Hell, ma'am, I'm just making damn sure there ain't no bees in this one."

———————————

A man turned to his buddy at a bar and said, "You know, I think self-abuse gets a bad rap."

"What do you mean?"

"Look at the shit you take to get some chick to spread her legs. If you masturbate, you can do it whenever you want, you know who you're dealing with, you know when you've had enough, and you don't have to be polite to some cunt afterwards."

The man and his wife were sitting in the marriage counselor's office. The counselor said to the man, "Your wife has been complaining that you totally ignore her sexual needs, that all you do is climb on and come two minutes later."

"Now, wait a minute, Doc," the man said. "I've tried. Last week I went down on her, just like she asked. But I'll tell you, I'll never do it again."

"Why not? Didn't she like it?"

"She liked it fine. But that was the problem. The goddamn pussy juice put my cigar out."

A woman walked into the drug store and said, "I want to buy a vibrator."

The druggist waggled his finger and said, "Come this way."

The woman replied, "If I could come that way, I wouldn't need a vibrator."

What's another name for masturbation?

I-balling.

Who won the prize for best costume at the literary costume ball?

The bottomless couple who came as Poe's *Pit And The Pendulum*.

Why isn't a woman like a volcano?

Volcanoes never fake eruptions.

What's the definition of a loser?

A guy to whom a hooker says she's got a headache.

A man was busy eating out his girlfriend when the telephone rang. Without moving she reached over and answered it. The call was from her mother, and they immediately got into an argument that went on for five minutes. Finally, the man raised his head and said, "Why the fuck don't you hang up on her?"

"Watch it," the girl snapped. "Just keep a civil tongue in my cunt."

A colleague at work took George aside and told him some rumors about his wife. That evening he arrived home early and told his wife he'd prepare dinner. But when she came into the dining room, she saw nothing but a head of lettuce on her plate.

"What's this?" she asked.

"I want to know if you eat like a rabbit, too," he replied.

———————

What's the best thing that comes out of a penis when you stroke it?

The wrinkles.

———————

What's the definition of a dildo?

A meat substitute.

———————

Why does Miss Piggy douche with vinegar and water?

Because Kermit likes sweet and sour pork.

What's a real loser?

A guy whose hand falls asleep when he's masturbating.

———————————

What's the difference between dark and hard?

It stays dark all night long.

———————————

Why are electric trains like a woman's tits?

They were originally intended for children, but it's the fathers who play with them.

———————————

Want to know what a woman goes through in childbirth?

Pull your lips back over your head.

———————————

Why is a sun-tanned girl like a roast turkey?

Because the white meat is best.

The two couples got together every Saturday night for years, and boredom had set in. One night, after several drinks, they decided to switch partners. The next morning, Harold woke up and said to his companion, "Did you enjoy that?"

"I had a terrific time," came the reply. "Let's go see how the girls did."

As a hooker was dressing, she turned to her customer and asked, "Have you just gotten out of prison?"

"Yeah," the guy replied. "How did you guess? Is it because I wanted to have sex from the rear?"

"Partly," she said. "But more because when we finished, you ran around in front of me, bent over, and shouted, 'Your turn.'"

A wino said to his buddy, "I'll never forget the first time I turned to drink as a substitute for women."

"What happened?"

"I got my dick stuck in the neck of the bottle."

A businessman was totally captivated by the ravishing redhead at the hotel bar. He was taken aback when she announced that her price was $500, but he was so horny that he agreed to pay.

They went upstairs to his room, and she headed into the bathroom. When she came back out, the man was lying naked on the bed, beating off furiously.

"What in the hell do you think you're doing?" she asked.

"Baby," the businessman panted, "for $500, you're not going to get the easy one."

After the company Christmas party, a vice president woke up with a gigantic hangover. He turned over and groaned to his wife, "What in the hell happened last night?"

"As usual, you made an ass of yourself in front of the chairman of the board."

"Piss on him," the man answered.

"You did," she said. "And he fired you."

"Fuck him," the man retorted.

"I did. You go back to work on Monday."

An influential politician was out driving in the country when his car got a flat tire and skidded into a ditch. He hiked to the nearest farm house, introduced himself, and persuaded the farmer to pull him out. The farmer got a big draft horse from the barn and led him out to the road. He hitched the horse to the car, and after a lot of effort got the vehicle on the highway.

The politician offered the farmer $5. The farmer looked at him hard, then whispered something to his horse. Immediately, the horse dropped his giant cock.

The politician was amazed. "I'll give you another five dollars if you tell me what you said to make the horse grow that hard-on."

The farmer grabbed the five, then said, "I told him that all politicians are cocksuckers."

The mailman came to the door with a small package addressed to Mr. Fred Ryan. His wife couldn't resist opening it, but she was revolted to find that the box contained a single large turd.

When her husband came home that evening, she told him the story, adding, "I can't imagine who sent that to us."

"I know," he said. "I've been expecting that tax return—shit from the government as usual."

A man got friendly with a woman at the hotel bar and took her to his room. They started to fool around, and soon he discovered that she had a huge cunt. Eventually, she took all her clothes off, lay down on her back, and spread her legs so wide she seemed ready to split.

The man looked at her and said, "Take it easy, babe. I generally fuck from the outside in, not the other way around."

———————————

The wealthy businessman was obsessed with marrying a virgin. He decided the only way to be certain was to adopt a six-year-old girl and wait until she was 18. He found an orphan and sent her to a monastery in Ireland to be raised.

Twelve years later, he brought the now ravishing young thing to America and married her. Carrying her into his bedroom, he put her gently on the bed, then pulled out a jar of Vasoline. "What's that for?" she asked.

"So I won't hurt you," he replied.

"You don't need that," she said. "Just spit on your cock like the monks did."

Two businessmen were in Las Vegas on business. One went back to his room to work after dinner, the other went out on the town. The man about town woke up the next morning with a phenomenal, paralyzing hangover. He did get himself together enough to discover his wallet was missing.

His friend offered to help, if he could remember where he was last. The guy thought, then said, "I remember a bar that was all gold. The walls were gold, the bar was gold, the glasses were gold, the writing on the cocktail napkins was gold—hell, even the urinal was gold."

"That should help," his friend said. And sure enough, a few inquiries produced a couple of possible clubs. The friend dialed one and asked the man who answered the phone if his club had gold walls and gold writing on the napkins.

"Yeah," the guy said.

"And what about a gold urinal?"

"Just a second," the man said. Then he called out, "Hey, Rufus, I got a lead on that drunken shithead who pissed in your saxophone last night."

————————————

What's brown and fuzzy and lays in the forest?

Smokey the hooker.

Why did the whore with two cunts get kicked out of the brothel?

The other girls didn't like her "holier than thou" attitude.

———————

Fred was desperately horny, but he only had five dollars. He went to the whorehouse anyway, and to his delight, the madam said she had a special in Room Five. Fred went up to the room and found a female rabbit. The rabbit dashed around for nearly ten minutes, but Fred finally caught it and got his satisfaction.

Fred got paid two days later and decided to return to the whorehouse for a more traditional thrill. This time the madam told him there was a special show in Room Six. He walked in to find another man staring through a two-way mirror as two women made passionate love in the next room. Fred watched for a while, then turned to his companion and said, "Hey, this is pretty good."

"You should have been here a couple of days ago," the man replied. "There was this crazy bastard catching and screwing a rabbit."

———————

The starlet was shouting at her agent, "You know I want to become a star. But there are some things I just won't do. Like that disgusting part that seventy-year-old producer offered me."

"What did you say when he offered you the part?"

"I laughed right in his balls."

Bill finally persuaded the curvaceous young secretary to go for a drive in the country. Unfortunately, the car got a flat tire in the middle of nowhere, and Bill had to climb out to change it. The February day was so bitterly cold that his hands became numb after five minutes. He got back in the car and stuck them between Anne's legs. She let out a scream, shouting, "What the hell do you think you're doing?"

"I have to warm my hands," he explained. "Or we'll never get back."

He got out of the car and five minutes later he came back in to warm his hands a second time. After a third stint the tire still wasn't changed. The fourth time he climbed into the car, he started to put his hands between Anne's legs when she turned to him and said, "Say. Are you sure your ears aren't getting cold?"

———————————

What's the difference between a vitamin and a hormone?

You can't hear a vitamin.

———————————

What is it that two men can do easily, a man and a woman with difficulty, and two women can't do at all?

Piss in the same pot.

Why does a cow have a long face?

If you had your tits pulled twice daily but were fucked only once a year, you'd have a long face, too.

———————————

What's indecent?

When it's in long, in hard, and in deep, it's in decent.

———————————

What is better than honor?

In 'er.

———————————

Why's a one-story brothel more profitable than a two-story brothel?

Because there's no fucking overhead.

———————————

What's the difference between a sin and a shame?

It's a sin to stick it in and a shame to pull it out.

What's the difference between frustration and utter frustration?

Frustration is the first time you can't do it a second time. Utter frustration is the second time you can't do it the first time.

Why is making love like a roll of toilet paper?

After you tear off the first piece the rest comes easily.

One woman said to another, "You look terrible this morning."

"I'm exhausted," the other admitted. "My husband won't go to sleep unless his hand is in my cunt."

"What's wrong with that?"

"He walks in his sleep."

One woman said to another, "How was your big date last night?"

She grimaced. "A big fizzle."

"The guy wasn't much in bed?"

"You ever try stuffing a marshmallow in a parking meter slot?"

"Sex is a drag," the woman said to her neighbor. "All that worry about getting pregnant."

"I thought your husband had a vasectomy?"

"He did. That's why I'm so worried."

_____

A young lady was so enamored of the cute kangaroo that she reached over the fence to pet it. Inadvertently, she grabbed the kangaroo's balls, and it went bounding over the fence and down the road.

The woman turned to a keeper who came running up and asked, "What did I do?"

"You squeezed that fucker's balls, lady," the keeper said. "And you better get ready to squeeze mine, because I've got to catch the son-of-a-bitch."

_____

What do they call a hooker's kids?

Brothel sprouts.

Chapter Eleven:

SIMPLY DISGUSTING

What do you do with dead baby twins?

Use one to swat the flies swarming around the other.

How do you play with a dead baby?

Cut off its arms and legs and use it as a football.

What do you call three dead babies piled one on top of another?

A stool.

What do you call four dead babies covered with glass?

A coffee table.

_____

What do you do when your baby dies on Thanksgiving?

Stuff the turkey with it.

_____

What do you have when you strap dead babies to each foot?

Slippers.

_____

How do you make a dead baby float?

Add root beer and a scoop of ice cream.

_____

Why is it easier to unload a truckload of dead babies than a truckload of bricks?

Because you can't unload bricks with a pitchfork.

The guy walked into a funeral home and said to the mortician, "I'll give you a hundred dollars for the vagina of the blonde laying in the casket in there."

The mortician looked at the guy as if he was nuts. "You're crazy. I could lose my license."

"What about two hundred?"

The mortician debated with himself, then said, "All right." He went in and cut it out. Then he shouted, "How should I wrap it?"

"That's okay. I'll eat it here."

———————————————

A man went into a barber shop to get a haircut and the barber found some curly blond hair in the guy's beard. So the man said, "That figures. Every morning I kiss my wife on the head before I go to work."

The barber started to laugh. "That doesn't explain why you have shit all over your necktie."

Two guys were fishing from a dock. One was pulling in one fish after another; the second had no luck at all. Finally the frustrated fisherman went over to the other guy and asked, "What in the hell are you using for bait?"

"Well," the second guy answered, "I know an undertaker. Everytime he gets a female stiff, he cuts off her pussy lips and puts them in a bucket for me. They make great bait."

"Pussy lips," the first guy remarked. He was silent for a moment, then asked, "Say, I notice that every time you take one of them out of the bucket, you put it up to your nose and smell it. Why?"

"Every once in a while that crazy bastard puts an asshole in here."

———————————

There was this couple marooned on a small island in the middle of the ocean, the only two survivors of a shipwreck. She was a virgin, but after a couple of months he convinced her that they were never going to be rescued, so she gave up her cherry. Two years later, though, she became so ashamed of what she was doing that she stopped eating and died.

A couple of years later, he became ashamed of what he was doing and buried her.

An airline passenger had to go to the bathroom badly, but the men's room was occupied. The stewardess, seeing his urgency, suggested he use the ladies' room. But she warned him not to press the buttons marked WW, WA, PP and A-T-R.

He got in and sat down, but his curiosity got the better of him. He pressed WW and immediately warm water washed over him. God, these women have it made, he thought. He pressed WA and warm air dried his ass. Then he tried PP, and a powder puff patted him gently with scented talcum. He was having such a good time he had to press A-T-R.

He awoke some time later in a hospital. He called the nurse, and asked, "What the hell happened to me? The last thing I remember I was in the ladies' room."

"You were," the nurse replied. "But you disobeyed the warning and pressed A-T-R. That stands for Automatic Tampon Removal. By the way, your cock is in a jar in the lab."

———————————

A man came into his friend's office and said, "Have you been listening to the radio?"

"No, what's up?"

"Good news and bad news. The bad news is that John Hinckley escaped from that mental institution."

"That's terrible. What's the good news?"

"Ronald Reagan's missing."

Ronald Reagan wrote a letter to John Hinckley after his trial.

Dear Mr. Hinckley:

Mrs. Reagan and I want you to know that after hearing the medical and psychiatric evidence presented at your trial, we agree completely with the verdict of not guilty by reason of insanity. Our whole family bears you absolutely no malice, and we wish you the very best success in your course of treatment.

Sincerely,
Ronald Reagan

P.S. We think you should also know that Tip O'Neill is fucking Jodie Foster.

A young man walked into an agent's office and announced that he could fart the "Star Spangled Banner." The agent told him to go ahead and give it a rip.

Before the agent knew what was happening, the young man had grabbed his waste basket and began shitting in it.

"Hey, what in the hell are you doing?" screamed the agent.

"Clearing my throat," the young man replied.

A young lady was explaining to her friend how the doctor had cured her hemorrhoids. "He bent me over his table," she said, "and then he put his left hand on my shoulder and stuck his finger up my . . . no . . . he had his right hand on my shoulder and stuck his . . . wait a minute . . . he had *both* hands on my shoulders!"

A man was sitting forlornly in the corner at a big party. A girl came over to him, sat down and said, "I've never seen anyone look so unhappy. What's wrong?"

The man said, "It's my career. I'm a composer, but no one will buy my music."

"You may be in luck," the woman said. "I'm a singer. Why don't you go play one of your songs for me."

The man went over to the piano and began to play a beautiful melody. The room grew quiet as the whole party listened. When the young man was finished, he was greeted with great applause. The singer rushed up to him, kissed him, and said, "That was wonderful. What's the name of your song?"

The young man replied, "It's called 'I Love You So Much I Could Shit In My Pants.'"

A man went to a whorehouse once a month and paid $200 for a girl. This time the madam told him she had something special for $500. The man almost backed out when he saw the girl wasn't any better looking than the $200 whores. Then the girl opened her legs and the tune "Hello Dolly" came out.

The man was amazed, and took the girl home for the night. He didn't fuck her, just sat listening. At five A.M. he called his best friend in New York and told him to listen. The girl's legs opened, and the song came out. When it was over, the man asked his friend what he thought. His friend snapped, "I can't believe you called me at this hour to hear some cunt sing 'Hello Dolly.'"

―――――――――――

The man and woman were going to a masquerade party. She came downstairs wearing only a lemon tied around her waist. He took one look, went upstairs, then came down wearing only a potato.

"What in the hell do you think you're doing?" she asked.

"Well, if you're going as a sourpuss, I'm going as a dicktator."

A middle-aged woman had always wanted to have a baby, but she couldn't get pregnant. She went to yet another doctor, who told her he couldn't give her a baby. But he could give her the experience of what it feels like to be pregnant. He put a cork in her ass and told her not to take it out for three months.

Three months later, the woman came back and said she felt all filled up, but she didn't feel like she had a baby inside. After six months she felt the same way. In her ninth month, she was in the shower one day when a monkey who'd escaped from a traveling circus came in the bathroom window. The monkey saw the cork and pulled it out. There was a gigantic brown explosion that blew the dazed woman off her feet. When she regained her senses, she saw the monkey, and grabbed it joyfully, saying, "You may be brown and hairy, but you're mine."

A man went to a whorehouse. When he started to screw a girl, his organ hurt, so he pulled it out and it was shorter. He was puzzled, but so horny that he put it back in. When it hurt again, he pulled it out to notice it was shorter still. He put his head on her lower stomach to investigate and heard a tiny voice cry, "More pork sausage, more pork sausage."

Bill found himself in a crush in the lobby of his office building. He started to fight his way to the front when he ran into a co-worker. "What's going on?" he asked.

"Some religious nut's in the elevator. He's soaked himself with gasoline and he's threatening to set himself on fire. I'm taking up a collection for him. Want to donate?"

"Sure. How much have you collected so far?"

"Eight books of matches and six lighters."

What's Preparation H?

Dingleberry jam.

What's a proctologist?

A crack investigator.

What's the difference between a beer and a booger?

A beer goes on the table, a booger goes under it.

The wife sat up in bed and asked her husband, "Why don't you ever go down on me?"

"I don't know," he said. "I just don't want to."

"Is it because you don't think my cunt is clean enough?" she demanded.

"What?" the husband said.

"I said, 'Is it because you don't think my cunt is clean?'"

"What?"

"Herb, are you deaf?"

"I'm sorry," her husband said. "The flies are buzzing so loudly I can't hear."

Ronald Reagan arrived in hell and was being shown around the place. When passing a pit full of unspeakable slime and filth, he saw all the Watergate crew. John Dean was covered up to his waist, Haldeman and Ehrlichman were submerged up to their necks. Next to them, John Mitchell was only knee-deep in the shit.

"Hey," the President said. "How come old Mitch rates such preferential treatment?"

"Don't worry about it," his guide said. "He's standing on Nixon's shoulders."

What did the man say when he came home to find his wife throwing up in the kitchen?

"Shit, leftovers again."

A drunk weaved his way into a coffee shop and asked another customer how he'd like a free steak, baked potato with sour cream, broccoli, apple pie a la mode, and coffee.

The guy said, "Great."

Then the drunk leaned over and threw up in his lap.

———————————

A kid came running into the kitchen to tell his mother that Daddy was throwing up all over the bathroom.

"Don't worry," she said. "Daddy can take care of himself."

"But Mommy," he said, "Jimmy's eating all the big pieces!"

———————————

Why are a woman's cunt and asshole so close together?

So when she gets drunk you can carry her home like a six pack.

The captain and some of his crew were returning to their ship after a night on the town. As they climbed up the ladder, the captain suddenly threw up all over himself and the men below. Pointing to the seaman above him, he shouted, "Give that man five days in the brig for throwing up."

The next day the captain found that the man had been given 10 days and he asked why. "Well," his mate said, "when we got you undressed, we found he'd shit in your pants, too."

———————————

A college student came back to the fraternity house one night raving about his date with a female weight lifter. "Come on," his friend said. "She's built like a refrigerator."

"Yeah, but she's a fantastic fuck. You've got to let me set you up with her."

Finally, the other student agreed. He arrived at the girl's dorm room, bottle of champagne in hand. He was surprised to see that she was already in her nightgown. He handed her the bottle. To his astonishment, she put it down in the middle of the floor and started to squat over it.

"Wait a second," the guy said. "I want to fuck the regular way."

"Sure," she said in her gruff voice. "But I thought you might want the cork pulled from that champagne bottle first."

A young virgin finally agreed to her boyfriend's pleading, but she was worried about the pain of that first encounter. She couldn't talk to her mother, but she got up the courage to consult her aunt, who told her not to worry. All she had to do was go to the butcher shop, buy a half pound of calf's liver and stuff it up her cunt. The liver would cut down on the pain and give the boyfriend such a good fuck that he'd go to sleep happy.

The virgin did as she was told. In the bathroom of the motel room, she stuffed the liver inside her, then went back to the bed. After an hour of heavy screwing, they both fell asleep. But when the girl awoke, she saw no sign of her boyfriend except a note on the pillow, which read, "I liked you a lot, but after seeing the mess on the bedcovers I threw up and had to leave.

"P.S. Your cunt's in the bathroom sink."

A man invited his girlfriend on a camping trip. They found a camp site after hiking all day, and he went out to forage for firewood. When he returned his girlfriend wasn't in sight. He was thirsty after his effort, but his canteen was empty. He rummaged in her knapsack, and found a rubber tube that seemed to be connected to a canteen. He's just started to sip when she came out of the bushes.

She stared at him in amazement for a moment, then said, "What in the hell do you think you're doing with my enema bag?"

142

The three car accident was so gory even hardened policemen were sickened. Everyone had been killed; blood was everywhere; one corpse was even decapitated. Before the cleanup, a drunk pushed his way through the crowd and told the police he recognized one of the cars as belonging to one of his friends.

The police were taken aback but let the drunk examine the bodies. He staggered over, picked up the severed head by its ears and looked it straight in the eyes. On the verge of puking, a cop managed to ask the drunk if it was his friend.

"Nope," the drunk answered. "My friend is taller."

———————————

Two nude marble statues—one a young girl, the other a young boy—stood a few feet away from each other in the park for nearly a century. One day the heavens above opened and a voice boomed out, "Statues. You've done your duty for the last hundred years. As a reward, I'm going to let you come alive for one hour."

A thunderbolt came down from heaven and the statues came to life. With looks of incredible lust, they rushed hand in hand to the bushes. For 55 minutes there came the sounds of grunting and groaning and thrashing. Finally, the voice boomed again, "Statues, you have five minutes left."

The boy turned to the girl and asked, "Do you want to do it one more time?"

"Yes," she replied, "but this time you hold the pigeon and I'll shit on it."

A young college student was standing outside the subway station, trying to cadge a token to get home. He wasn't having any luck until an ugly older woman came up and told him with a leer that she had a token up her cunt, and that if he could get it out with his teeth, he could keep it. The thought repulsed the young man, but after another ten minutes of fruitless panhandling, he gave up.

They went down an alley and he began chewing away, more enthusiastically as time went on. Finally his tongue found something hard. He was so excited that he ran down the alley, into the subway station, and dropped the token in the slot. He started to push through when a transit cop stopped him.

"Hey, Mac," the cop said. "What in the hell do you think you're doing trying to use a scab instead of a token?"

A guy was coming on to a beautiful chick in a bar who seemed to be responding enthusiastically. When the guy went to the men's room to take a piss, another patron stopped him and said, "I thought I'd tell you. That chick has also got a man-sized cock."

Instead of being turned off, the guy was excited. He hustled the chick out of the place, got into the car, and drove out to an isolated spot. They started to get it on, then the chick excused herself to take a piss. The guy waited a minute, then snuck out to follow her. Sure enough, he saw this big round long thing hanging down between her legs. So he ran up beside her and grabbed it.

She jumped. "I didn't know you were back there!" she exclaimed.

"No," the guy said in a disgusted voice, "and I didn't know you were taking a shit, either."

———————————

A man named George had some strange sexual fetishes, the most bizarre of which was sucking pus. One night he searched around the city's sleeziest streets until he found a hooker who admitted to having a boil between her cunt and her asshole. Gleefully he paid her price and took her to a hotel room.

She spread her legs and George went right to work sucking pus. After a little while, she couldn't control herself and she pissed. He drank the piss. A little while later, she felt like shitting, so he rubbed the shit all over himself. Then, without warning, she let out a huge fart.

George looked up and barked, "What are you trying to do, bitch, gross me out?"

A husband and wife were lying in bed playing fart football. The husband went first, laying down a long, wet one. "7-0," he said.

The wife produced an equally gross blast. "7-7," he said.

The game went on until the husband took a 28-21 lead. The wife strained to tie, her face reddening at the effort. Instead of farting, she shit on her side of the bed. For a moment, she didn't know what to do. Then her face brightened and she announced, "Halftime. Change sides."

———————————

Every night the husband came home drunk and threw up in the sink. And every night his wife told him one day he'd puke his guts out. Finally, to teach him a lesson, she cleaned a couple of chickens and left the innards in the sink.

Sure enough the husband came home totally plastered and headed for the kitchen as usual. After a very long time, the husband staggered into the bedroom and plopped down on the bed. To his wife's delight, he turned to her and said, "You know you were right, honey. I've got to stop this puking my guts out."

"I told you so," she said.

"Yeah," he said. "Fortunately, using your long-handled spoon, I got my guts back in."

Did you hear about the guy who chewed his baby's toes off?

He forgot his wife was pregnant.

———————————

How do you tell if a girl is wearing pantyhose?

When she farts, her ankles swell.

———————————

A woman went into a bar and ordered a glass of whiskey. As she picked up the drink, her hand shook so badly she kept spilling it. The bartender commented, "Boy, you sure are nervous this morning, lady."

"That's nothing," she said. "You should have seen me last night. I tried to douche and ended up giving myself an enema."

A rancher came into the Nevada brothel with a sad story about most of his calves being killed by coyotes. All he had left was five dollars to get laid. The madam said, "Don't worry, we've got a five dollar special down the hall."

The rancher opened the door to see a great looking brunette with huge tits lying on her back, legs open, waiting for him. He tore off his clothes, climbed on, and pumped away for dear life.

All of a sudden, when he came, come started oozing out of her nose and eyes and asshole and cunt. The rancher raced down the hall to tell the madam. She told him not to worry and called to her doorman, "Sam, the dead one's full again."

The bereaved husband was standing in the funeral home next to his wife's casket, greeting friends and relatives. Finally, his older brother came up and told him they had to talk in private. When they got out into the hall, the brother said, "Everybody's gossiping like crazy. Why in the hell did you choose a Y-shaped casket for Margaret?"

"Well," the man said, "I came home and found her nude in bed. For once she wasn't bitching that she had a headache, so I took off my clothes and climbed on. It wasn't until rigor set in that I noticed she was dead, and then it was too late to get her legs together."

Two explorers were lost in the Sahara desert. They went for two days without food and water, and they were near death when they saw buzzards circling ahead of them. Gathering their strength, they came upon the remains of a dead camel. One explorer was so hungry he rushed forward and gorged himself on the rotting flesh as his disgusted comrade looked on. A few minutes later, the overeager man crawled away from the carcass and started to vomit.

"Ah hah," his friend said, leaping forward. "Just what I've been waiting for. A hot meal!"

———————

There were two fleas on a woman. One crawled in the front door, and one went around and in the rear. The next morning the front flea asked the rear flea, "How did you sleep?"

"Not bad," the rear flea responded. "But every once in a while I was awakened by a very foul south wind. How did you sleep?"

"Great, at first. Then some bald-headed bastard stuck his head in the window and puked all over me."

———————

A couple lay in bed after two hours of heavy entertainment. "Did you enjoy it?" he asked. "The sex, the vibrator, the enema."

"Yeah," she said. "I always like it at the time. But why do I always have to sleep on the brown spot?"

A guy walked into a brothel with only $5. All the madam could offer him for that amount of money was a wax job.

"What in the hell is a wax job?" he asked.

"Do you want it or not?"

The guy said yes, handed her the $5, then followed her upstairs to a room where a nude hooker waited. He could feel himself get hard as she undid his pants. Then she led him over to the window, laid his cock down on the sill, and slammed the window shut so hard the wax flew out of both ears.

———————————

A man walked up to the complaint desk of a department store and said, "I'm furious at you people. This shotgun I bought for my brother-in-law doesn't work."

The complaint department manager took the shotgun for a moment, examined it, then flicked a switch. "There," he said. "You didn't disengage the safety catch."

The man took the gun back, looked at it for a second, then squeezed the trigger. The blast blew a six-inch round hole in the complaint manager's chest. The corpse fell to the floor in a pool of blood and gore.

The man looked over the counter for a moment, then shook his head. "Shame," he muttered. "Guy was a smart fucker."

To Bill's surprise, his wife announced she was pregnant. They agonized for so long over whether to have the baby or not that when they finally decided a kid was too much of a hassle, no doctor would perform the abortion. So Bill went to work with a coat hanger. There was blood all over the bathroom before his wife finally started to get contractions. Ten minutes later, the fetus dropped into the toilet.

"There," his wife said with a monumental sigh of relief. "At last it's over."

"Wait a second," Bill cried in a frenzied tone. "We've made a terrible mistake."

"What do you mean?"

"I think it had my nose!"

———————

Two friends set up a laboratory in a garage to invent a product that would make them both millionaires. But all they had was a string of spectacular failures. Finally, one Saturday Fred came running out of the lab screaming, "Bill, I got it! I've got it! We're rich."

"What is it?" Bill asked.

"The invention of the century. It's a chocolate chip cookie that tastes like pussy."

"A chocolate chip cookie that tastes like pussy?" Bill repeated skeptically.

"Man's two favorite foods. Come on, try it."

Bill followed Fred into the lab, where he was handed a large dark brown cookie. He took a big bite, then wrinkled his nose in disgust. "God damn it, this tastes like shit."

Fred came over to take a look. Then his expression brightened and he said, "I know what's wrong. Turn it over. You're eating the wrong side."

The girl asked her date, "What do you think of anal sex?"

"Ugh!" the guy exclaimed. "I couldn't stick my prick up anyone's rear unless I was stone drunk."

"The whiskey's in the top left cabinet," she said.

The guy had a fetish for hairy women. The not-so-faint mustache on the heavyset woman sitting at the bar drove him wild. After several drinks, they went back to her apartment. When she took off her blouse, he was thrilled to see that she had huge growths under her armpits. He ran his hands through the hair as she took off her panties, then turned his attention to her fabulous bush.

She watched him impatiently for a moment, then said, "Listen, Mac, I brought you here to fuck, not to knit."

Private Smith was ordered by his sergeant to go down to the river and get drinking water. He went off, then came running back. "Sarge," he said, "there's a big alligator in that river."

The sergeant put a hand on his shoulder. "Son, that alligator is four times as scared of you as you are of it."

"Sarge, if that alligator is only half as scared, that water's not fit to drink."

Charlotte suddenly developed a heart problem and the doctor said that she had to have total quiet and rest in a nursing home. Shortly after her confinement, her husband Larry began an affair with a ravishing waitress twenty years younger. After four months, however, the waitress told Larry she was going to withhold her affections unless he made her an honest woman and married her.

Larry debated for a couple days, then his libido got the best of him. He bought a package of firecrackers, figuring he'd sneak up to his wife's window, place the firecrackers on the sill, then light the fuse. The shock was sure to do her in.

He waited until it was dark, then was putting his coat on when a cab pulled in the driveway. To his amazement, his wife got out of the vehicle and walked slowly toward the door. He rushed out and said, "Charlotte, what are you doing?"

"I can't take that nursing home. I'm coming home to die."

"Thank God," Larry said. "I was afraid I'd have to go to the home and kill you."

───────────

An American on safari was in a jeep that stopped in a remote African village. He was taking a drink of water with his African guide when he saw a gorgeous young white woman walk out of a tent. "Who's that?" he asked.

"The daughter of the missionary, Bwana."

"Boy," the horny American said, "I'd sure like to eat her."

The African quickly raised his rifle and shot her.

The new American ambassador was being entertained by an African diplomat. They'd spent the day discussing what the country had received from the Russians before the new government kicked them out.

"The Russians built us a power plant, a highway, and an airport. Plus we learned to drink vodka and play Russian roulette."

The American frowned. "Russian roulette's not a very nice game."

The diplomat smiled. "That's why we developed African roulette. If you want to have good relations with our country, you'll have to play. I'll show you how."

He pushed a buzzer, and a moment later six magnificently built, nude black women were ushered in. "You can choose any one of those women to give you oral sex," he told the American.

"That's great," the ambassador said. "That doesn't seem much like Russian roulette."

"Oh, it is. One of them is a cannibal."

The small traveling circus was going bankrupt fast. The owner tried a dozen desperate schemes to draw more customers, but nothing worked until he persuaded the elephant trainer to finish his act by catching an elephant turd on a plate and eating it with a knife and fork.

The prospect of seeing a man eat a plate of elephant shit brought farmers from fifty miles around, filling the circus tent to the seams. The spotlight was on the elephant trainer and the drummer gave a big flourish as the big dark turd plopped on the plate. A pretty girl tied an apron around the elephant trainer's neck and he sat down. Then he put his knife and fork down.

A huge chorus of boos came from the crowd. The circus owner rushed up and the trainer said, "I can't eat this disgusting stuff."

"You have to," the owner said. "Besides, you've done it a dozen times in rehearsal."

"Yes," the trainer said. "But look. The shit's got a hair in it!"

———————————

The foot said to the penis, "I have a terrible life. My owner sticks me in a stinky shoe and treads on me all day."

"You think that's bad," the penis said. "My owner sticks me in this dark hole that smells like fish and makes me do push-ups until I throw up."

What do you call a rubber sheet?

A golden shower curtain.

––––––––––

What do you call a penis?

A golden shower rod.

––––––––––

What do you call a cunt?

A golden shower spray.

––––––––––

A man walked into a bar and asked for ten shots of whiskey. The bartender lined them up, and the man proceeded to down all ten in about two minutes. After he was done, the bartender asked him, "Hey, what was the occasion?"

"I just got my first blow job."

The bartender said, "Great, let me buy you another shot of whiskey."

"No," the man said. "If ten shots won't kill the taste, nothing will."

Two ladies were out driving in the Virginia countryside fifty miles from Washington, D.C. One of them pointed out two naked men in a field masturbating each other. "Look," she said, "two Democrats jerking each other off."

"How do you know they're Democrats?" her friend asked.

"If they were Republicans, they'd be fucking a crowd of poor people."

———————

After the plane reached cruising altitude, the plane's captain came on the intercom with the usual announcement welcoming the passengers, giving their cruising altitude and speed, and estimating arrival time. Not knowing the microphone button had stuck, the captain turned to his copilot and said, "I think I'll go take a shit and fuck that new stewardess."

Naturally, everybody on the plane heard. As one of the stewardesses ran forward to inform the captain, an old lady grabbed her arm and said, "No need to rush, dearie. He said he was going to take a shit first."

———————

What did the seven dwarfs say when the handsome prince awakened Snow White?

"I guess it's back to jerking off."

Why do scientists think women are descended from mermaids?

Because they smell like fish below the waist.

_____

What song did the mermaid sing to the sailors?

"I can't give you any thing but head, baby."

_____

Cinderella was very happy for a while after marrying the handsome prince, but eventually she became bored. She started fooling around, and soon she was screwing everything in pants. Her fairy godmother warned her several times, to no avail. Finally, she became so upset that with a wave of her wand she turned Cinderella's cunt into a pumpkin.

Two weeks later, the fairy godmother checked in. She was amazed to see Cinderella looking happier than ever. "What happened?" the fairy godmother asked.

"I've just met Peter Peter," Cinderella replied.

_____

A guy went into the sex shop to look for artificial vaginas, but he was appalled at the price. "What do you mean charging $30 for a few cents' worth of latex and a few dollars' worth of vibrator?"

"You can't look at it that way," the shop owner said. "That's a hole that's worth a lot more than the sum of its parts."

During World War II, a high-ranking American officer was arrested by MP's while being given a blow job by a female Nazi spy. He was court-martialed on charge of insertion in the face of the enemy.

_____

What's the difference between kinky and perverted?

A guy who's kinky brushes his cock with a feather; a pervert fucks the whole chicken.

_____